Showcase 500
beaded jewelry

Showcase 500
beaded jewelry

Photographs of Beautiful Contemporary Beadwork

Ray Hemachandra

LARK
CRAFTS
Asheville

JUROR AND SENIOR EDITOR
Ray Hemachandra

EDITOR
Julie Hale

ART DIRECTOR AND COVER DESIGNER
Matt Shay

ART PRODUCTION
Kay Holmes Stafford

FRONT COVER
CLOCKWISE FROM MAIN IMAGE
Betty Stephan
Cathedral Windows, 2010

Amy Katz
The Wonder Wheel, 2010

Suzanne Golden
Polka Dotty, 2011

Betsy Youngquist
Eye Heart Pendants, 2011

BACK COVER
CLOCKWISE FROM TOP LEFT
Melanie Potter
Pining Over You, 2010

Faith Wickey
Bowtie Leaf Pendant, 2010

Rebecca R. Starry
High-Caliber Collar, 2009

Ileana Munteanu
Mystic Flower Brooch, 2011

Kathleen E. Wade
Spinning Bead Ring, 2011

SPINE
Diane Hyde
Time Warped, 2009

FRONT FLAP
Paulette Baron
Rainforest Pendant, 2010

BACK FLAP
Melissa Ingram
Magic Carpet Ride Cuff, 2011

OPPOSITE
Kira Seiden
Cube Necklace, 2010

TITLE PAGE
Katharina Eder
Fadenspiel Rainbow Necklace, 2011

LARK CRAFTS

An Imprint of Sterling Publishing
387 Park Avenue South
New York, NY 10016

If you have questions or comments
about this book, please visit: larkcrafts.com

Library of Congress Cataloging-in-Publication Data

Hemachandra, Ray.
Showcase 500 Beaded Jewelry : Photographs of Beautiful Contemporary Beadwork / Ray Hemachandra. — First Edition.
     pages cm — (500 series)
ISBN 978-1-4547-0316-7 (pbk.)
1. Beadwork. I. Hemachandra, Ray. II. Title: Showcase five hundred beaded jewelry.
  NK3650.S55 2012
  745.58'209051—dc23

                2012001139

10 9 8 7 6 5 4 3 2 1

First Edition

Published by Lark Crafts
An Imprint of Sterling Publishing Co., Inc.
387 Park Avenue South, New York, NY 10016

Text © 2012, Lark Crafts, an Imprint of Sterling Publishing Co., Inc.
Photography © 2012, Artist/Photographer

Distributed in Canada by Sterling Publishing,
c/o Canadian Manda Group, 165 Dufferin Street
Toronto, Ontario, Canada M6K 3H6

Distributed in the United Kingdom by GMC Distribution Services,
Castle Place, 166 High Street, Lewes, East Sussex, England BN7 1XU

Distributed in Australia by Capricorn Link (Australia) Pty Ltd.,
P.O. Box 704, Windsor, NSW 2756 Australia

Manufactured in China

ISBN 13: 978-1-4547-0316-7

For information about custom editions, special sales, and premium and corporate purchases, please contact the Sterling Special Sales Department at 800-805-5489 or specialsales@sterlingpub.com.

Requests for information about desk and examination copies available to college and university professors must be submitted to academic@larkbooks.com. Our complete policy can be found at www.larkcrafts.com.

contents

introduction

This book is a testament to a community, a conversation, and a phenomenal body of jewelry artwork.

Beading, one of the world's oldest forms of creative expression, professionalized in recent decades with the artwork and books of leading beaders—and particularly beadweavers—like Virginia Blakelock, Carol Wilcox Wells, and Diane Fitzgerald. But the advent and power of social media have changed the development of the beading community and its collective body of work entirely.

Every day online, beaders communicate and commune. They exchange ideas and tell tales of their beading spaces, obsessions, and foibles. They share personal stories of daily family life, meals, illness and recovery, and deaths. They talk about their etsy stores, design copyright, classes, and travels and about all the joys, toils, and minutiae of workaday life.

Most of all they share photographs of their beadwork and they support each other. They celebrate one another's designs and achievements. They offer constant words of encouragement, support, and love. The development and expansion of the beading community in recent years is a story of empowerment, of friendship, and of family.

The artistic community and the conversation are now global. Beaders from all over the world participate, contribute, and belong.

Some of the voices and personalities are constant and formidable. But the online medium also holds space for the quiet, unsure ones to post an image now and then and a request: "Look." And they get flooded with the same clicks of approval and words of support, which reach them as personally in their home studio as from a friend in their living room or a peer in a local bead shop. Like many social and cultural groups, the online beading community provides a sense of identity, place, and even validation and worth. And when beaders get together in person—whether at a national or regional bead show or at a local bead shop—it's often like meeting for the very first time people they already know intimately, or seeing once more annual friends who are more like dearly missed relatives.

JEAN POWER
Geometric Beaded Beads ■ 2009

Showcase 500
beaded jewelry

The book includes so many beaders with wonderful personal stories to share and that I'd like to share ... but this isn't *that* book. That's another book to come soon, I hope. This book instead tells its stories through its photographs of jewelry, the innovative expressions of these women and men who use beads, filament, wire, and fabric to share their creative voices.

Those voices are incredibly diverse and, appropriately for the book's global reach, they speak in different languages. The 500 pieces of jewelry presented reflect the popularity of beadweaving, certainly, as evidenced by the use of almost every stitch known to humankind, but also of bead embroidery, quilling, loom weaving, and kumihimo braiding, as well as basic stringing, simple wirework, and fine metalwork. Many pieces from outstanding bead makers are included, too, such as a flameworked bead showcased in a straightforward jewelry setting.

This collection includes work from many of the world's best-known beading artists—the superstars and the master designers and teachers—and it also presents pieces made by talented beaders whose work has not been published previously. More than 360 artists from 30 countries submitted photography of their

JENNIFER WELLS
Ripple ■ 2011

jewelry for consideration in this book, and I think the enthusiasm, energy, and creative juice of today's global beading community are captured here. The designs are brilliantly inventive, beautiful, and often surprising.

A book like this one typically takes two years to make, from drawing board to execution to the finished books arriving in brick-and-mortar and online stores. So the work shown on these pages mostly suspends a moment in time: All of these photos could instead have been posted on Facebook ... and then new work from the artists would have followed in the days, weeks, and months afterward. The work constantly matures, expands, crystallizes, and flows.

Still, honestly, this book thrills me. It tells the story of a now fully developed artistic community with both striking design visions and ambitions and an irrepressible yet heart-centered personality. I think it will be a mainstay on the coffee tables and bookshelves—including yours—of many beaders, jewelers, crafters, and art fans for years to come.

I hope you enjoy seeing all the inspiring pieces these photos capture—and that you can sense all the stories, passion, commitment, and hard work the artists express in their jewelry.

— **Ray Hemachandra**

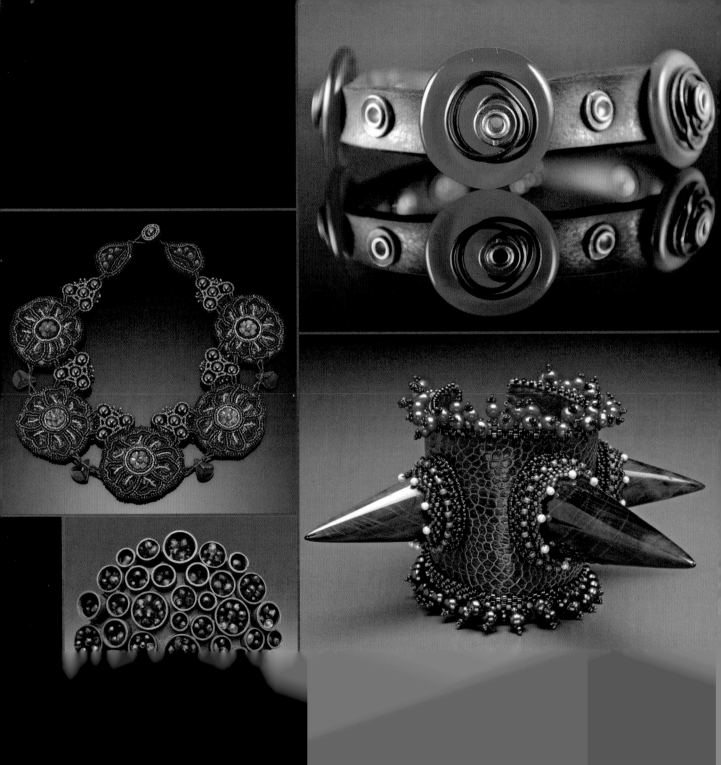

the jewelry

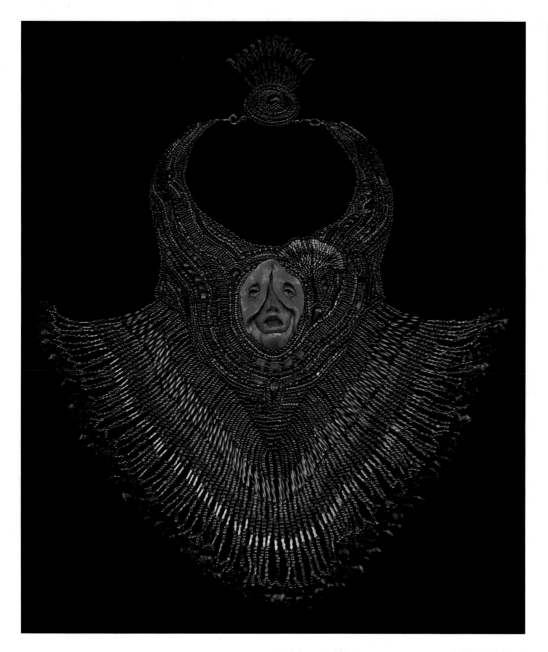

DIXIE GABRIC
Do You Really Know Me? ■ 2011
21 x 14 cm
Ceramic face, seed beads, pearls;
peyote, backstitch, brick, layering
PHOTOS BY JEFF GABRIC

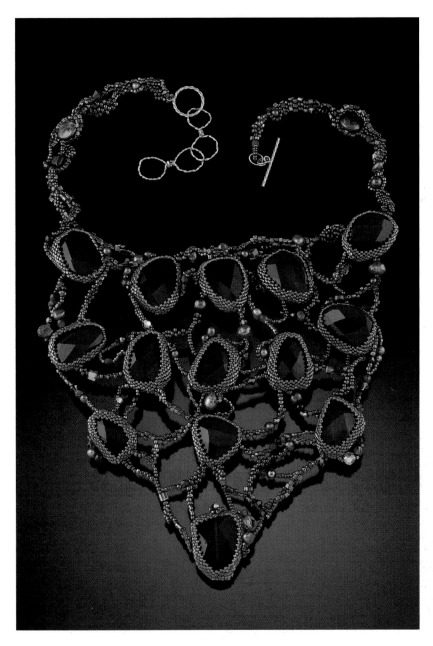

RACHEL WEISS
Carnelian Necklace ■ 2010

45.7 cm wide
Carnelian gemstones, seed beads,
pearls; bead embroidery, peyote
PHOTO BY LARRY SANDERS

11

AMY KATZ
Athena's Muse ■ 2011

3.8 x 0.8 x 44 cm
Seed beads, Tila bead crystals, glass pearls;
peyote, square, right-angle weave
PHOTO BY CARRIE JOHNSON

HELENA TANG-LIM
Infinity ■ 2009

Pendant: 5.5 x 3 cm
Seed beads, crystals, magatamas; Ndebele
PHOTO BY ERIC LIM

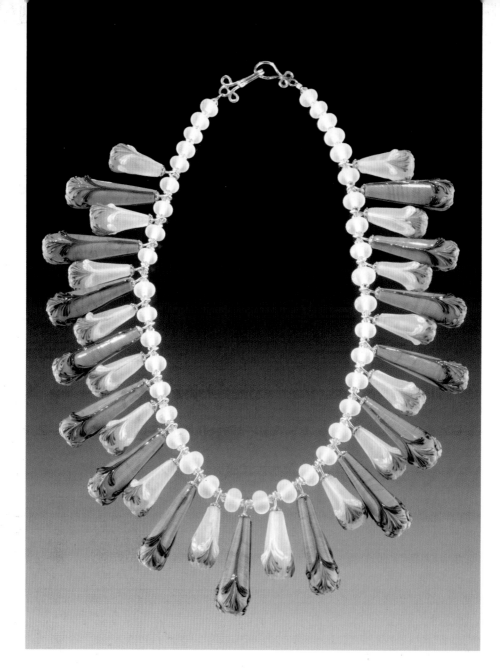

PATRICIA ZABRESKI
Necklace for Queen Nefertiti ■ 2010

50.8 x 5.1 x 1.3 cm
Handmade lampworked glass beads,
etched lampworked beads, Swarovski
crystals, handmade sterling clasp

Showcase 500
beaded jewelry

BETTY STEPHAN
Cathedral Windows ■ 2010

33 x 28 cm
Glass cabochons, stone cabochons, crystal cabochons,
metal findings, glass beads, seed beads; bead embroidery
PHOTO BY TIM FUSS

15

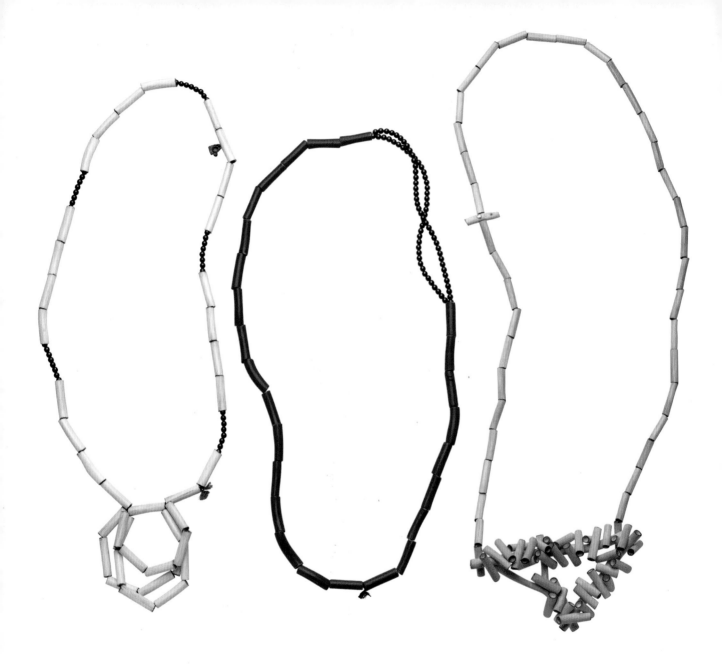

JULIE BLYFIELD
White and Black Loop Desert Acacia Neckpiece, Rust Quandong Stick Neckpiece, and *Native Frangipani Stick Neckpiece* ■ 2009
35 x 14 x 2 cm; 33 x 12 x 0.5 cm; 40 x 12 x 4 cm
Desert acacia wood, quandong wood, native frangipani wood, sterling silver, paint, silk thread, wax; oxidized
PHOTO BY GRANT HANCOCK

Showcase 500
beaded jewelry

NANCY MELI WALKER
Coexist Prayer Beads ■ 2011
60 x 8 x 2.5 cm
Sterling-silver beads and clasp, rosewood rosary, Buddhist
rudraksha seed prayer beads, Islamic Tasbih sandalwood prayer
beads, leather necklaces; chased, fabricated, assembled
PHOTO BY STAN SHOLIK

BETSY YOUNGQUIST
Eye Heart Pendants ■ 2011

Each: 13 x 13 x 0.9 cm
Seed beads, coral beads, turquoise beads, bugle beads,
antique glass beads, vintage glass stones, antique
glass doll's eyes, pewter heart finding; mosaic
PHOTO BY LARRY SANDERS

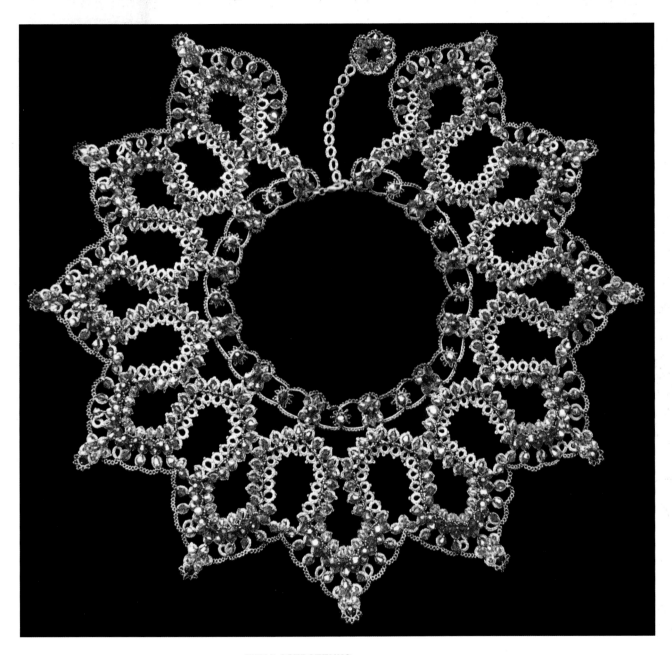

IRINA ASTRATENKO
Venera ■ 2010
40 x 40 x 0.8 cm
Seed beads, Swarovski crystals, thread
PHOTO BY ARTIST

HEIDI KUMMLI
Earth Spirit ▪ 2011
30.5 x 20.3 x 1.3 cm
Seed beads, cabochons, vintage buttons,
leather, mesh, ermine tails; bead embroidery
PHOTOS BY ARTIST

SUE HORINE
The Raven ■ 2011

30.5 x 19 cm
Porcelain raven, Deschutes jasper cabochon,
amber and black onyx cabochons, seed
beads, brass dangles; bead embroidery
PHOTOS BY ARTIST

21

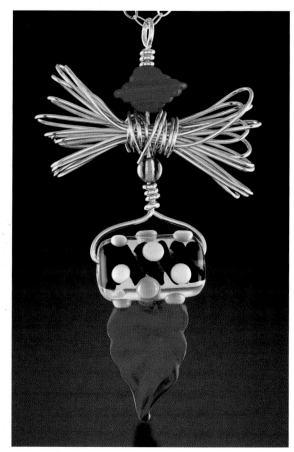

SANDY LENT
Anemone Pods ■ 2011
6.4 x 40.7 x 6.4 cm
Lampworked beads, acid-etched beads,
acid-etched lampworked rounds; strung
PHOTO BY RYDER GLEDHILL

FAITH WICKEY
Bowtie Leaf Pendant ■ 2010
7.5 x 5 x 8 cm
Lampworked glass bead,
sterling silver; wirework
PHOTO BY LARRY SANDERS

TERESA SULLIVAN
Whirling Dervishes Lariats ■ 2007

Each: 101 x 5 x 5 cm
Seed beads, acrylic glass, pressed glass,
stone, trade beads; peyote, stringing
PHOTOS BY ARTIST

MARCY ANTLE
Silver Queen ■ 2011
38 x 22 x 3 cm
Seed beads, pearls, buttons,
metal pieces; bead embroidery
PHOTO BY LISA BARTH

FACING PAGE
SUZANNE GOLDEN
Ring around the Daisy ■ 2011
4 x 13.5 cm
Seed beads, acrylic beads;
tubular, spiral peyote
PHOTO BY ROBERT DIAMANTE

Showcase 500
beaded jewelry

LAURA MCCABE

Blue Goldstone-Eye Mace Necklace ■ 2010

Pendant: 4.5 x 4.5 x 4.5 cm; length of necklace: 45 cm
Glass doll's eye, blue goldstone points, glass seed
beads, crystal beads, freshwater pearls; peyote,
herringbone, lacy stitch, embellishment

PHOTOS BY MELINDA HOLDEN

VANESSA WALILKO
Dreams of the Fallen ■ 2008

25 x 43 x 25 cm
Seed beads, bugle beads, onyx, agate, hematite,
iolite, blue goldstone, tektites, upholstery vinyl, velvet;
bead embroidery, hand stitched, tubular peyote
PHOTO BY LARRY SANDERS

KIRA SEIDEN
One Necklace, Four Different Ways of Wearing ■ 2007

32 cm long
Glass beads, Murano glass

29

KERRY D. VINE
Entomologist's Dream ■ 2011
45 x 10 x 1 cm
Seed beads, insect-wing coverings, baroque
pearls; freeform netting, freeform peyote, fringe
PHOTO BY TOM HASSLER

PRISCILLA MARTIN
Egret's Garden a.k.a. Home Sweet Home ■ 2011

31.5 x 33 cm
Lampworked glass beads, lampworked glass buttons,
effetre glass, seed beads, silk, wool thread, wire
PHOTOS BY SCOTT WILD AND ARTIST

SHERRY SERAFINI
Spring Fling ■ 2009
30.5 x 16.5 cm
Crystals, felt, sequins, seed beads
PHOTOS BY ARTIST

TAMUNA LEZHAVA
1001 Nights ■ 2011

49 x 3 cm
Seed beads, Swarovski beads and crystals,
chains, metal-covered beads; right-angle weave,
tubular Ndebele, square, square Ndebele
PHOTO BY VAKHTANG ALANIA

33

CAROLINE GORE
...harnessing... ■ 2011
15 x 5 x 1.3 cm
Sterling silver, spinel, jet,
hematite, silk; oxidized
PHOTO BY ARTIST

JANE BOHAN
Lure ■ 2011
Each: 6.4 x 1.9 cm
Poly-celluloid beads, billiard-ball acrylic beads,
18-karat white gold, 18-karat yellow gold, sterling
silver, diamonds; CAD/CAM, milled, hand fabricated
PHOTO BY HAP SAKWA

EVE ALTA EDMONDS
Tribal Bracelet ■ 2009
14.5 x 1.5 cm
Indian-head nickel, millefiori beads,
wax cotton cord; strung
PHOTO BY MARTIN BARKER

JOSEPH NASKAR
Peyote Trilobite 450 m.y.o. ■ 2010
5 x 19 x 0.9 cm
Delica beads, 450-year-old trilobite
fossil, lava-stone clasp; two-needle
odd-count peyote, right-angle weave
PHOTO BY ARTIST

MELISSA BLAND
Stria Necklaces ■ 2010
Each bead: 6 x 5.7 x 0.6 cm
Copper bead: stoneware, iron oxide; cone 10, reduction
Black bead: stoneware with underglaze; cone 10 reduction
White bead: raw porcelain, cone 10 oxidation
PHOTO BY JOHN POLAK

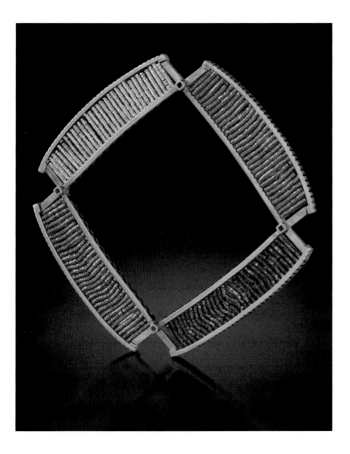

SHARON M. DONOVAN
Skinny Bangle Bracelet ■ 2011

4.5 x 4.5 x 0.3 cm
Sterling silver, hex metal beads;
fabricated, woven
PHOTO BY LARRY SANDERS

JANE-MICHAEL STALLINGS
Rolly Chain ■ 2010

66 x 10 cm
Seed beads, chain, sterling silver; peyote
PHOTO BY AMANDA LANGORIA

KAREN BACHMANN
Ice Cube Necklace ■ 2010

50 cm long
Acrylic, rock crystal, sterling silver;
carved, polished, strung
PHOTO BY RALPH GABRINER

FRANCINE WALKER
Glacial Pools ■ 2010

28 x 20 x 1 cm

Sterling silver, aquamarine beads, amazonite beads, quartz beads, white agate
beads, yellow turquoise beads, lime jade beads, freshwater pearl beads,
blue topaz, peridot; hammered, soldered, riveted, bezel set, wire wrapping

KATHY KING
*Art Deco Bead Quilled
Necklace* ■ 2010

43.2 x 12.7 x .6 cm
Seed beads, glass beads; quilling
PHOTO BY JASON DOWDLE

ANN TEVEPAUGH MITCHELL
Christo in Central Park ■ 2006
31 x 25 x 1.5 cm
Seed beads, thread; peyote
PHOTO BY DEAN POWELL

41

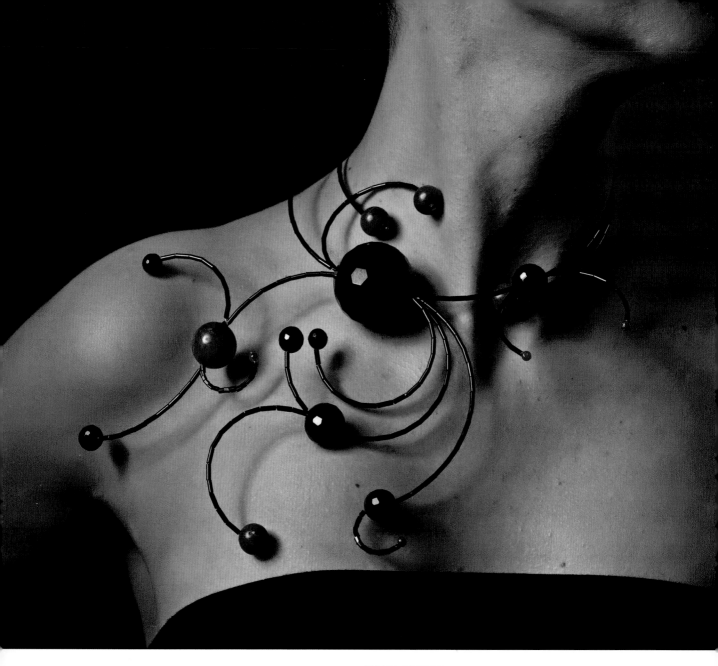

JULIA DUSMAN
Tarantula ■ 2011
23 x 23 x 3.5 cm
Black onyx, coral, carnelian, glass beads, memory wire
PHOTO BY JENS LOOK

JANE-MICHAEL STALLINGS
Sacred Heart Lei ■ 2009

78 x 7.5 cm
Seed beads; Dutch spiral, peyote
PHOTO BY AMANDA LONGORIA

43

MARGO C. FIELD
Fan Dance Necklace and Earrings ■ 2011
Necklace: 21 x 16 x 1.5 cm; earrings: 3 x 4 x 1 cm each
Seed beads, crystals, glass pearls, pewter
beads, silver wire; herringbone, peyote, fringe
PHOTOS BY PAT BERRETT

MARCIA DECOSTER
Dancing Light ■ 2011

25 x 15 x 1 cm
Seed beads, crystals, Swarovski crystal,
element pearls; ladder stitch
PHOTO BY ARTIST

CAROLE HORN
Neptune's Garden Necklace ■ 2009

24.1 x 24.1 cm
Seed beads; herringbone, peyote
PHOTO BY D. JAMES DEE

CAROLE HORN
Manhattan Flower Garden Necklace ■ 2010

24.1 x 24.1 cm
Seed beads; herringbone, peyote, various stitches
PHOTO BY D. JAMES DEE

WENDY ELLSWORTH
Chakra Spiral ■ 2011

53 x 3 x 3 cm
Seed beads; gourd
PHOTO BY DAVID ELLSWORTH

JOANN BAUMANN
Triangles Bracelet ■ 2009

11 x 11 x 3 cm
Delica seed beads; peyote
PHOTO BY LARRY SANDERS

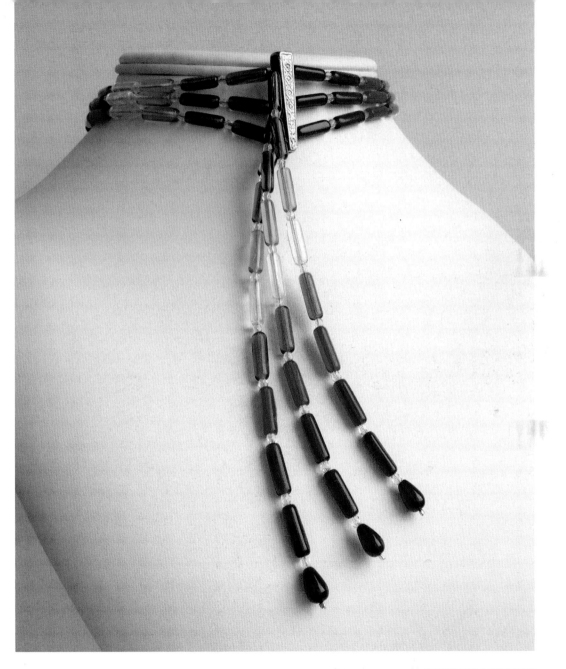

CATHARINA THOMAS
After the Rain Necklace ■ 2010
16 x 11 x 11 cm
Glass beads, crystals, magnetic clasp; stringing
PHOTO BY ARTIST

49

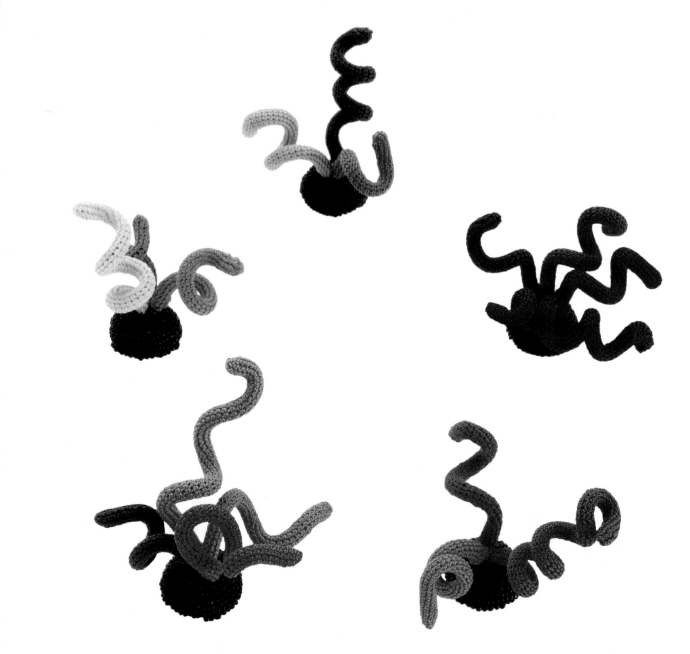

KATHARINA EDER
Fadenspiel Mobile Necklace ■ 2010

Each part: 5 x 5 cm
Mobile elements, magnetic necklace
PHOTO BY SIMONE ANDRESS

KERRIE SLADE
Warrior Queen ■ 2010
20 x 3 x 2.5 cm
Seed beads, cylinder beads, fire-polished
beads; peyote, netting, herringbone
PHOTO BY ARTIST

DHARMESH KOTHARI
NAMRATA KOTHARI
Mogul Endless Bead Rings ■ 2009
Each: 3.8 x 2.2 x 1.8 cm
Amethyst, citrine, 18-karat yellow gold
PHOTO BY KEVIN CHUNG

BRONWEN HEILMAN
Concho Bracelet ■ 2011

3 x 20 cm
Glass, recycled bicycle inner tube, steel, spent
rifle shells, sterling silver, enamel; flameworked
PHOTO BY MAYA HAWK

BRONWEN HEILMAN
Recycled Bottle-Glass Ring ■ 2010

3 x 3 x 2 cm
Glass, recycled bicycle inner tube, steel, spent
rifle shells, sterling silver, enamel; flameworked
PHOTO BY DAVID ORR

TAMARA SCOTT
Summertime ■ 2010

Each: 5 x 8.5 cm
Seed beads, crystals, pewter, gemstones, ceramic
beads, abalone, wood, turquoise; netting, peyote
PHOTOS BY ARTIST

53

MARY DIMATTEO
Pearl Bracelet ■ 2011

22.5 x 1.5 cm
Freshwater pearls, fire-polished beads, seed
beads, gold charlottes; spiral-stitch variation
PHOTO BY ROBERT DIAMANTE

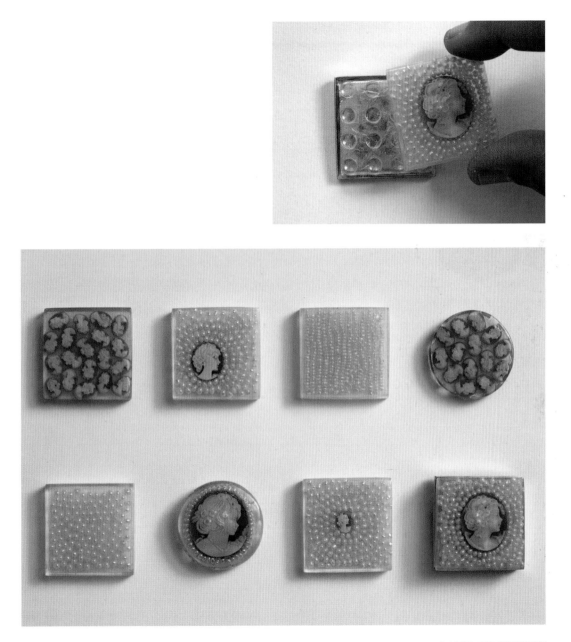

DANIA CHELMINSKY
Deconstructed Cameos ■ 2011

Various dimensions
Natural pearls, carved cameos, epoxy
resin, silver; fabrication, casting
PHOTOS BY RAN ERDE

MYRA E. SCHWARTZ
Mermaid's Gift ■ 2009
55.9 x 5.1 x 3.2 cm
Antique Meerschaum mermaid pipe, antique natural coral, lampworked glass,
glass beads, freshwater pearls, sterling-silver beads, mermaid toggle, coated wire; strung
LAMPWORK BY MAUREEN HENRIQUES
PHOTO BY ARTIST

JUDIE MOUNTAIN
WAYNE ROBBINS
Serendipity ■ 2010

70 cm long
Torchworked glass, copper metal clay, Czech glass, brass,
branch pearls, horsehair; sculpted, hand formed
PHOTOS BY PAUL SCHRAUB

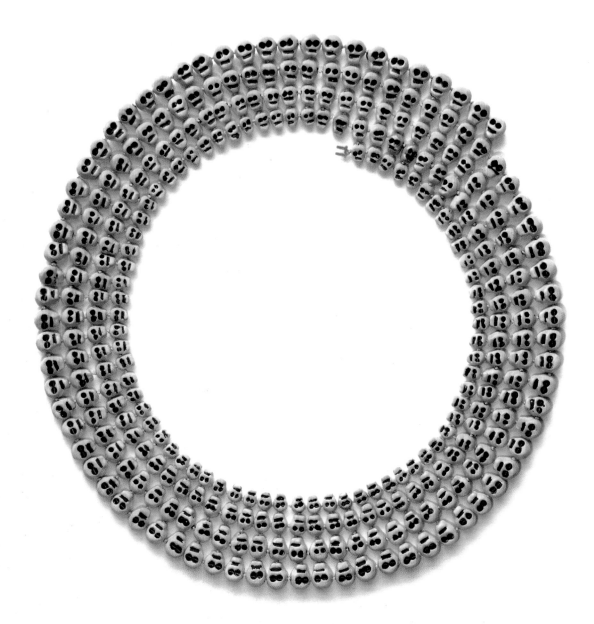

PETER HOOGEBOOM
Infinite Collar ■ 2010
35 x 35 x 1.1 cm
Ceramics, nylon, alpaca; hand fabricated
PHOTO BY ARTIST

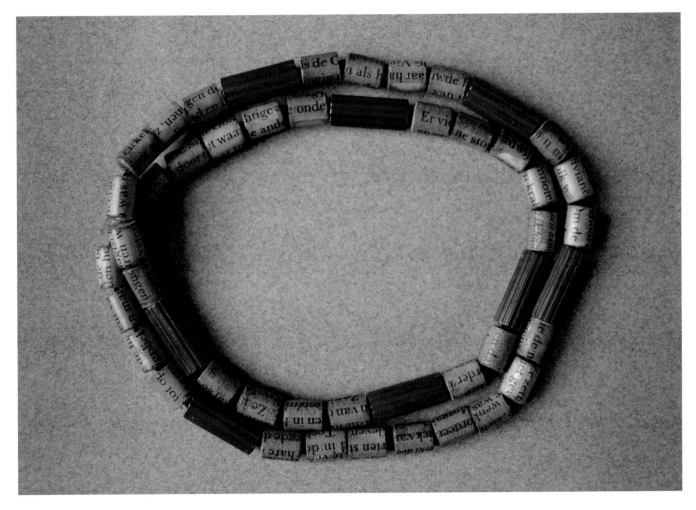

INGEBORG VANDAMME
Story Necklace ■ 2006

23 x 23 x 1.2 cm
Brass, paper, paraffin
PHOTOS BY ARTIST

JAN HULING
Cicada Necklace ■ 2011
43.2 x 4.4 cm
Seed beads, crystals, metal; glued
PHOTOS BY PHIL HULING

JAN HULING
Summer Leaves ■ 2011
58.4 x 6.4 cm
Seed beads, metal; glued
PHOTO BY PHIL HULING

61

**JUDIE MOUNTAIN
WAYNE ROBBINS**
Necklace ■ 2009

76.2 cm long
Lampworked glass beads, pietersite,
Baltic amber, sterling silver, fine silver

SHER BERMAN
Forty-Seven ■ 2006

50.8 cm long
Lampworked glass beads, freshwater
pearls, sterling silver, soda-lime glass

HARTMUT WUTSCHKE
Stop and Go ■ 2010
47 cm long
Lampworked beads, rubber, linen
PHOTOS BY MANUELA WUTSCHKE

DIANE HYDE

Time Warped ■ 2009

38.1 cm long
Seed beads, glass pearls, crystal bicones, chain,
vintage watch parts, charms, stampings, porcelain face,
suede-like material; bead embroidery, peyote, stringing
PHOTOS BY ARTIST

KAREN J. LAUSENG
Fishing Swivel Necklace ■ 2010

40 cm long
Fishing swivels, sterling-silver jump rings
PHOTO BY ARTIST

ELHADJI KOUMAMA
Tuareg Crosses on Silver and Onyx Beads ■ 2010
Various dimensions
Fine silver, black onyx; hand
engraved, lost wax method

DIANE FITZGERALD
Tilla Tepe Necklace ■ 2010
45.7 cm long
Charlotte-cut seed beads, Delica cylinder beads,
wooden beads, thread; peyote, netting

MELANIE POTTER
Pining Over You ■ 2010

40 x 20 cm
Seed beads, magatamas, faceted
stones; chevron chain, peyote
PHOTO BY SCOTT POTTER

67

KAREN PAUST
Liquid Sunset ■ 2009
17 x 18 x 4 cm
Seed beads, wool; crocheted, fulled
PHOTO BY ARTIST

KAREN PAUST
Pea Pod ■ 2011
11 x 2.5 x 2.5 cm
Seed beads, cotton, linen,
sterling silver; crocheted
PHOTO BY ARTIST

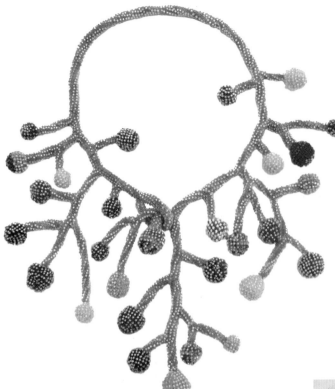

KAREN PAUST
Spun Sugar ■ 2009
25 x 21 x 2 cm
Seed beads, wool; hand
dyed, crocheted, fulled
PHOTO BY ARTIST

RHONDA UPPINGTON
Cherry with a Hint of Lime ■ 2011
53 cm long
Felt beads, seed beads, glass beads, metal
spacers, seed beads; hand stitched, wet felted
PHOTO BY ARTIST

69

MARSHA WIEST-HINES
Bollywood Beauty ■ 2010

38 cm long
Cylinder beads, seed beads, crystals; triangle
weave, peyote, netting, herringbone, fringe
PHOTOS BY ARTIST

MARY ANN HELMOND
Jackson Pollock ■ 2011
Earrings: 5 x 3.5 cm each; necklace: 56 x 6 cm;
ring: 2.3 x 2.6 cm; bracelet: 21.5 x 4 cm
Hollow lampworked beads, seed beads,
sterling-silver findings; stringing
PHOTOS BY THOMAS WRIGHT

71

AURELIO CASTAÑO
Jardin del Sol Ring ■ 2011

6.4 cm in diameter
Fire-polished crystals, rivoli beads, Delica beads,
Swarovski crystals; peyote, netting
PHOTOS BY JAMES KATT

Showcase 500
beaded jewelry

KATHRYN BOWMAN
Ah Gosh ■ 2011

55.9 cm long
Czech pressed-glass beads, fire-polished glass beads,
seed beads, Swarovski crystals, Chinese crystals,
sterling-silver closure, beaded beads; wire wrapping
PHOTO BY ANNIE PENNINGTON

73

DEBRA WARD (design)
KANDRA NORSIGIAN (beading)
Amulet Purse Necklace ■ 2000

15 x 5 cm
Seed beads, crystals, vintage Czech
drops; herringbone variation
PHOTO BY STEVE ROSSMAN

JENNIFER CAMERON
Carnival ■ 2011

27 x 16 x 2 cm
Sterling silver, lampworked
hollow beads; forged
PHOTOS BY KEN RIEVES

75

JAMIE CLOUD EAKIN
Bling! ■ 2011
19 x 10.2 cm
Crystals, rivolis, fire-polished
beads, seed beads; bead
embroidery, herringbone rope
PHOTO BY BRIAN JAMES

CARRIE JOHNSON
Curvaceous Bull's-Eye ■ 2007
21.5 x 3 x 1.5 cm
Seed beads, freshwater pearls, gold-filled
rings and clasp; peyote, embellished
PHOTO BY ARTIST

KARMEN L. SCHMIDT
Breastplate I: Treasure Chest ■ 2010

26 x 21 x 2 cm
Swarovski crystal stones, Swarovski crystal bicones and faceted rounds, crystal
sequins, seed beads, charlottes; peyote, square, chevron, netting, Ndebele,
right-angle weave. stitch-in-the-ditch, basket capture, embellishment
PHOTOS BY TERESA SULLIVAN

77

JOANN BAUMANN
Golden Elemental Collar ■ 2009

20 x 18 x 3 cm
Delica seed beads, handmade
glass beads; peyote
PHOTO BY LARRY SANDERS

KIMBERLY STATHIS
Sea Nettles Necklace ■ 2009

55.9 cm long
Seed beads, Swarovski crystals and pearls; off-loom beadweaving
PHOTO BY MARTIN KONOPACKI

KAREN BETTIN
Samba ■ 2011
43.2 cm long
Seed beads, crystals; horizontal netting
PHOTOS BY ARTIST

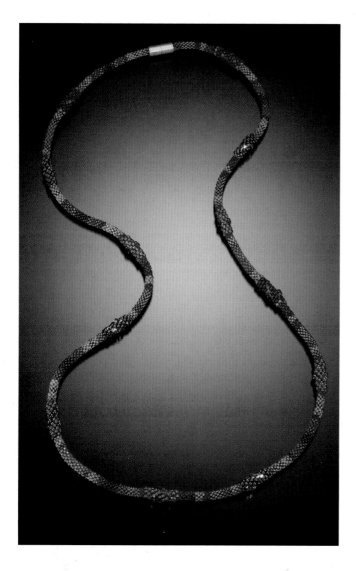

LYNNE SAUSELE
Warm Tone Beaded Cord Necklace ■ 2011

107 x 0.8 x 0.8 cm
Seed beads, sterling-silver
magnetic clasp; bead crochet
PHOTO BY ROBERT DIAMANTE

SHERRY LEEDY
Polka-Dot Agate Bracelet ■ 2010

13.3 x 12.7 x 3.2 cm
Seed beads, agate, onyx, coral, cerulean
beads, glass beads; round peyote
PHOTO BY E. G. SCHEMPF

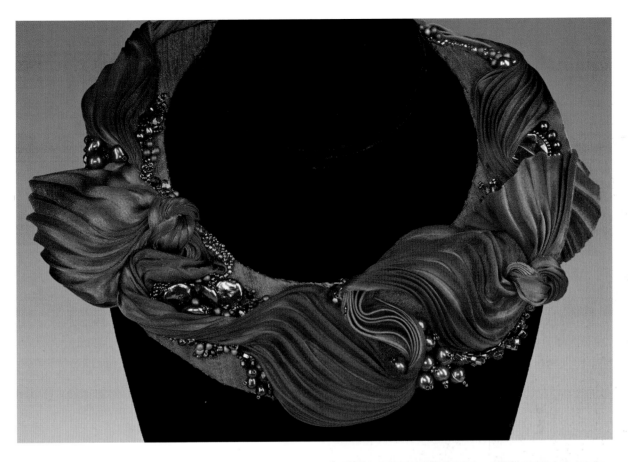

LAURIE DANCH
Autumn Ribbon Collar ■ 2010

17.5 x 21 x 1.3 cm
Dupioni silk, silk shibori ribbon, seed beads,
crystals, pearls; bead embroidery, peyote
PHOTOS BY MARTIN KONOPACKI

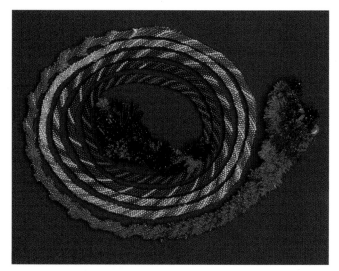

JEANNETTE COOK
Ra the Sun God Necklace ■ 2008
76 x 7 x 0.5 cm
Beads, electrical-wire armature
PHOTO BY MELINDA HOLDEN

VIRGINIA L. BLAKELOCK
Crocheted Rope Necklace ■ 2008
150 cm long
Seed beads, bugle beads; bead crochet, fringing
PHOTO BY GARY LEE BETTS

ELIZABETH RUSNELL
Yellow Irregulars ■ 2010

40 x 6.5 x 4 cm
Handmade porcelain beads, polymer beads, seed beads,
cotton cord; knitted, macramé, fringe, embellishment
PHOTO BY JOE JUSTAD

83

TAMARA SCOTT
Juliet ■ 2010
7 x 20 cm
Seed beads, pearls, turquoise, fabric, leather, resin, glass,
bronze flowers, original artwork; bead embroidery, brick
PHOTO BY ARTIST

FACING PAGE
TERESA SULLIVAN
Ecstasy ■ 2005
40 x 46 x 25 cm
Seed beads; peyote
PHOTO BY DAN KVITKA

DEBRA EVANS-PAIGE
Perpetual II ■ 2011
100 x 1.6 x 1.6 cm
Porcelain; hand formed, textured, oxidation fired
PHOTO BY DANIEL DINSMORE

KARIN ROY ANDERSSON
A Constant Grinding ■ 2011
Various dimensions
Gum base, softeners, sweeteners, flavorings, potato
flour, pearl silk, silver, chewed beads; tied
PHOTO BY ARTIST

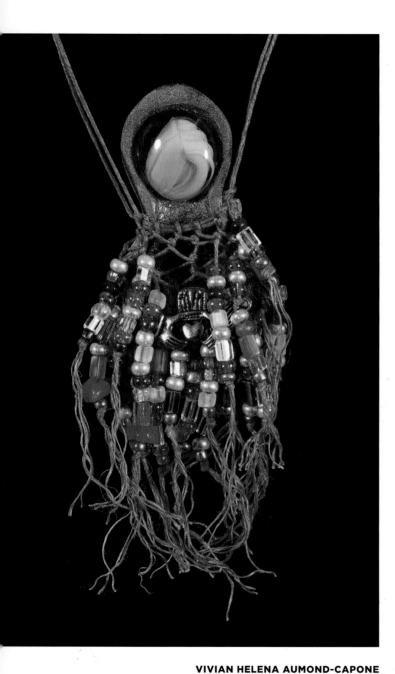

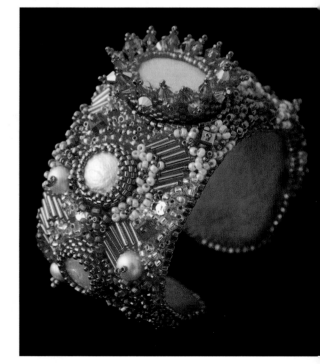

VIVIAN HELENA AUMOND-CAPONE
Heart and Hands ■ 2010
11 x 4 x 3 cm
Miniature jewelry gourds, seed beads,
wax linen, found objects, metal charm;
painted, knotless netting, wrapping
PHOTO BY DAVID HOFFMAN

SANDY TALLY
Green with Envy ■ 2009
3.8 x 21 cm
Seed beads, bugle beads, pearls, crystals,
rhinestones, lemon chrysoprase, suede-like fabric,
brass blank; bead embroidery, peyote
PHOTO BY BRIAN HUTSON

CARRIE JOHNSON
Ocean Depths ■ 2008

7 x 3.5 x 2 cm
Seed beads, Venetian glass, Swarovski
crystals, freshwater pearls, sterling-silver
beads and toggle; freeform peyote
PHOTO BY ARTIST

CARRIE JOHNSON
Tantalizing Twists ■ 2011

Each: 5.5 x 1.5 x 1.3 cm
Seed beads, Swarovski crystal, gold-filled findings
PHOTO BY ARTIST

BARBARA SCOTT-FISHER
Flower Arrangement Pendants ■ 2009

Left: 7.4 x 3 x 1.7 cm; right: 8.4 x 5 x 1.5 cm
Lampworked glass beads, seed beads,
crystals, coral, turquoise, enamel,
metal, plastic, wire; woven
PHOTO BY RALPH GABRINER

FELIEKE VAN DER LEEST
Peace Parrot ■ 2010

14 x 10 x 2.5 cm
Textile, seed beads, gold-plated metal,
plastic animal, gold, cubic zirconia;
bead crochet, needlework
PHOTO BY EDDO HARTMANN

NANCY SCHINDLER
Carnevale ■ 2011

40.6 cm long
Porcelain, pewter, seed beads, glass, stone, silk, thread,
copper; hand built, kiln fired, wirework
BUTTERFLY BEADS BY GREEN GIRL STUDIOS
PHOTO BY ARTIST

LUCIE VEILLEUX
Five Stars ■ 2010
18 x 10 x 4 cm
Torrefied birch, onyx beads,
stainless-steel wire, lobster clasp;
cut, pierced, polished, threaded
PHOTO BY ARTIST

LESLIE ROGALSKI
Dragon Cuff ■ 2011
16 x 4 x 4 cm
Cylinder beads, seed beads, Swarovski crystals, snap closure;
two-drop peyote, brick, flat right-angle weave, picot embellishment
PHOTO BY ARTIST

ANDREA L. STERN
Pod People ■ 2008

45 x 12 x 6 cm
Seed beads, Swarovski crystals, wire; peyote
PHOTO BY MARTIN STERN

LAURA MCCABE
Ostrich Cuff ■ 2010

16 x 6.5 x 6.5 cm
Custom-cut tiger's-eye points, seed beads,
freshwater pearls, ostrich-leg leather, grommets;
bead embroidery, peyote, embellishment
PHOTO BY MELINDA HOLDEN

REBECCA R. STARRY
High-Caliber Collar ■ 2009
25 x 29 x 2 cm
Seed beads, accent beads, bullets, findings;
right-angle weave, off-loom stitches

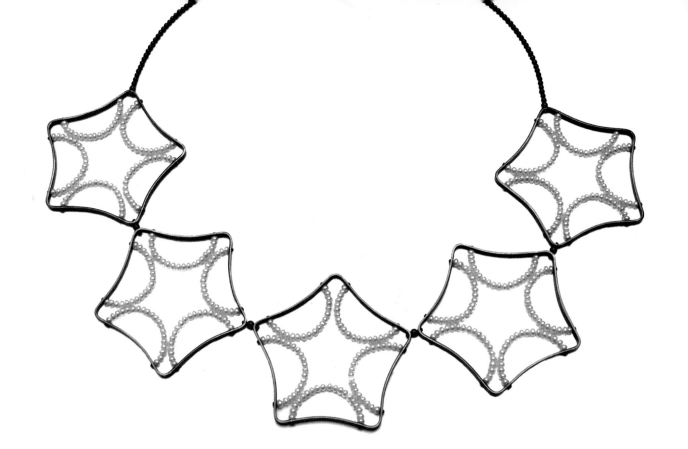

BIRGIT LAKEN
Hoya Camosa Buds ■ 2010
20 x 24 cm
Pearls, blood coral, silver; oxidized
PHOTOS BY ARTIST

BIRGIT LAKEN
Hoya Camosa Pendant ■ 2010

9 cm wide
Blood coral, pearls, silver; oxidized
PHOTO BY ARTIST

ESTEFANIA R. ALMEIDA
Ebb and Flow ■ 2011
9.5 x 44 x 0.4 cm
Bead rivets, nylon, plastic
PHOTOS BY HECTOR OLGUINI

CHRISTINE GUIBARA
Tourmaline Necklace ■ 2010
75 x 3 cm
Tourmaline beads, watermelon
tourmaline slices, 14-karat
gold; wire wrapping
PHOTO BY ARTIST

VALERIE BROWN
Roseate Waves ■ 2008
38 cm long
Seed beads, crystals, pearls, rose quartz,
glass focal bead, silver wire; twisted tubular
herringbone, right-angle weave, netting, wirework
PHOTO BY PAUL AMBTMAN

CARLA BRONZINI
Collana Mare ■ 2010

30 x 25 x 2.5 cm
Seed beads, crystals, pearls, stones,
mother of pearl; right-angle weave
PHOTO BY ARTIST

CARLA BRONZINI
Collana Madreperle ■ 2010

25 x 18 x 2 cm
Mother of pearl, pearls; beading
PHOTO BY ARTIST

PETER HOOGEBOOM
DNA Necklace ■ 2010

43 x 22 x 1.5 cm
Ceramics, nylon, beads; hand fabricated
PHOTO BY ARTIST

PETER HOOGEBOOM
Pebble Jugs Necklace ■ 2011

34.5 x 34.5 x 0.9 cm
Ceramics, cork, nylon, hollow
beads; hand fabricated
PHOTO BY ARTIST

CHEQUITA NAHAR
Kwasibita Necklace ■ 2010
56 x 20 x 2.5 cm
Porcelain beads, cord; knotted
PHOTO BY GALLERY MARZEE

CHEQUITA NAHAR
Okraai Klara Necklace ■ 2010
98 x 22 x 2.8 cm
Pinewood beads, porcelain beads, cord
PHOTO BY GALLERY MARZEE

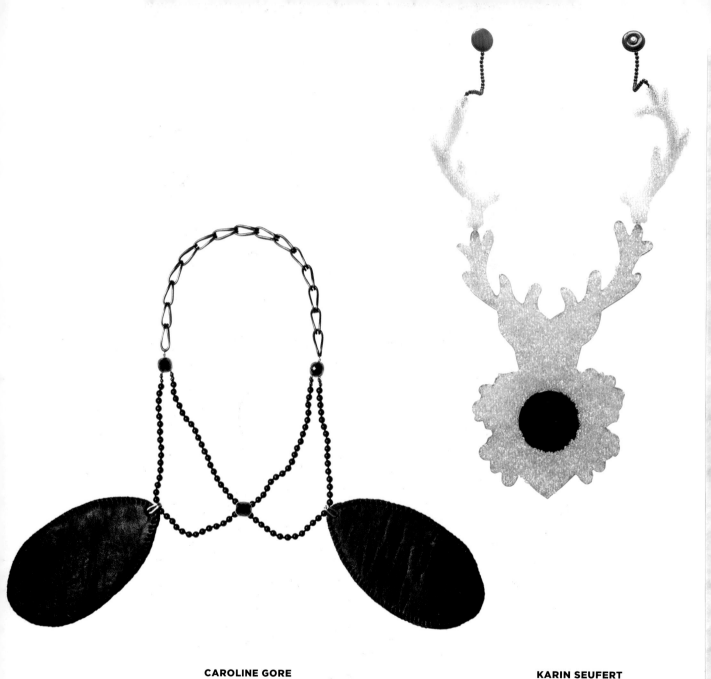

CAROLINE GORE
...double opaque... ■ 2011
27 x 29 x 1 cm
18-karat gold, sterling silver, black spinel,
jet, reclaimed leather, silk; oxidized
PHOTO BY ARTIST

KARIN SEUFERT
Necklace ■ 2004
30 x 14 x 0.8 cm
Silver, glass beads, onyx, lacquer;
crocheted, bead embroidery
PHOTO BY ARTIST

MELISSA BORRELL
Silhouette Dress ■ 2011

91.5 x 38 x 12.7 cm
Vintage glass pearls, thread;
freeform beading
PHOTO BY JACK ZILKER

ILEANA MUNTEANU
Mystic Flower Brooch ■ 2011
7 x 5.5 x 0.5 cm
Mother of pearl, seed beads, rivoli
crystals, pearls; peyote, bead lace

SUSAN BLESSINGER
Impending Bloom ■ 2011
16 x 16 x 1 cm
Seed beads, Czech fire-polished beads, Swarovski crystal,
antique tricycle reflector, copper washer, precision-
mechanized gears, vintage sequins, gunmetal ball chain
PHOTOS BY TODD KEITEL

SUSAN TERESE MCKECHNIE
Button Down ■ 2010
Various dimensions
Seed beads, vintage mother-of-pearl buttons,
freshwater pearls, fire-polished glass, suede-
like fabric; bead embroidery, peyote, fringe
PHOTO BY TOM VAN EYNDE

Showcase 500
beaded jewelry

MARGO YEE

Lyrical Flourish ■ 2011

22.9 x 19.1 x 1.9 cm

Seed beads, cube beads, glass beads, Venetian glass beads, lampworked leaves, enamel leaves, copper wafer, copper disc, copper flowers, metal flowers, pearls, quartz, cut glass, buttons, copper beads, flamed beads, epoxy clay; strung, riveted

GLASS LEAVES BY DONNA NOVA; ENAMEL LEAVES BY NORDIC GYPSY
PHOTO BY VALERIE SANTAGTO

LUCIA NIEVES CORTÉS
Imagined Heirlooms: Genesis ■ 2010

Various dimensions
Seed beads, silver, silk;
embroidery, bead embroidery
PHOTO BY W. IMILAN

LUCIA NIEVES CORTÉS
Imagined Heirlooms: Genesis ■ 2010

Various dimensions
Seed beads, silver, silk;
embroidery, bead embroidery
PHOTO BY W. IMILAN

ANNA BELOM
Labradorite and Sapphire Necklace ■ 2009

29.5 x 1.6 x 0.7 cm
Labradorite, sapphire, 14-karat gold-filled chain, 14-karat
gold-filled wire, 14-karat gold findings; wire wrapping
PHOTO BY ARTIST

ISOLINA PEREZ
Eclipse Necklace ■ 2007

Pendant: 8 x 6 x 1 cm
Scenic jasper, labradorite, green garnet,
fine silver; crochet, wire wrapping
PHOTO BY PETER CLOUGH

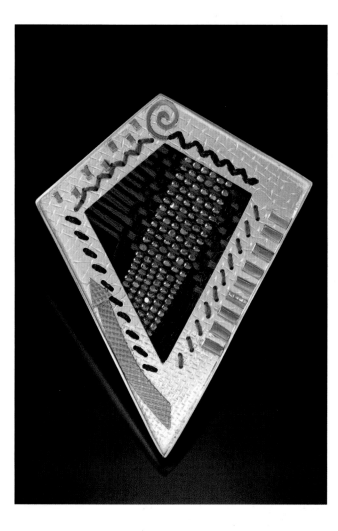

SHARON M. DONOVAN
Past Tapestry IV ■ 2009

3 x 2 x 2.5 cm
Sterling silver, 14-karat gold, glass beads,
silk thread; fabricated, woven
PHOTO BY LARRY SANDERS

TOP
L. SUE SZABO
Shadow Boxing ■ 2007

18.7 x 4.5 x 0.2 cm
Vintage metal seed beads, sterling silver;
hand fabricated, riveted, peyote
PHOTO BY ERICA CRISSMAN

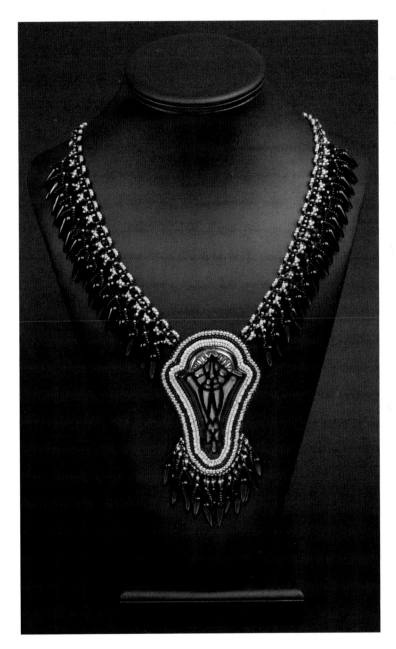

JENNIFER VANBENSCHOTEN
Bracelet ■ 2005

3.2 x 7 cm
Cylinder beads, faux suede,
aluminum cuff; peyote, brick
PHOTO BY SHERWOOD LAKE PHOTOGRAPHY

JENNIFER VANBENSCHOTEN
Glamour and Goth ■ 2010
Centerpiece: 12 x 6.3 cm
Handmade ceramic cabochon, onyx drop beads, fire-polished
beads, seed beads; bead embroidery, loop fringe, double flat spiral
PHOTO BY SHERWOOD LAKE PHOTOGRAPHY

ANNELIESE HAUPTSTEIN
From the Deep Necklace ■ 2008
52 x 1.6 x 0.8 cm
Sterling silver, kangaroo leather, freshwater pearls;
rapid prototyped, hand assembled, finished
PHOTO BY ARTIST

PAULETTE BARON
Rainforest Pendant ■ 2010

29 x 8 x 5 cm
Seed beads, Swarovski crystals
and pearls; peyote
PHOTO BY CARRIE JOHNSON

KATHLEEN E. WADE
Eight-Options Bead ■ 2011

2.1 x 2.1 x 0.7 cm
22-karat gold, 18-karat gold, Argentium sterling silver, spessartite
garnet, steel cable; fabricated, pierced, welded, bezel set
PHOTOS BY GEORGE POST

RACHEL NELSON-SMITH
You & Eye ■ 2009
28 x 26 x 1.5 cm
Glass, crystal, nylon, leather, silver; lampwork, bead
embroidery, peyote, herringbone, fringe, wirework
LAMPWORK BY RONIT DAGAN
PHOTO BY ARTIST

FACING PAGE
KATHARINA EDER
Fadenspiel Rainbow Necklace ■ 2011
16 x 1 x 47 cm
Antique seed beads,
polyamide thread; bead crochet
PHOTO BY SIMONE ANDRESS

VANESSA WALILKO
Dragon Lady ■ 2006
71 x 28 x 25 cm
Seed beads, silver box clasps;
off-loom beadweaving
PHOTO BY TREAVOR DOHERTY

PATTY HABERMAN
Thief Necklace and Brooch ▪ 2011

Necklace: 30 x 18 x 2 cm; brooch: 12 x 13 x 5 cm
Seed beads, wooden beads, felt, embroidery floss,
wood, paint; tubular peyote, bead embroidery
PHOTOS BY DAVID ORR

CANDICE ST. JACQUES
Sleeping Volcano Bracelet ■ 2011

3.1 x 21.3 cm
Opaque mosaic glass round, mosaic glass tile, seed beads,
bugle beads; right-angle weave, peyote, herringbone
PHOTOS BY EDDY ANTHONY

YVONNE CABALONA
Atlantis ■ 2010
Pendant: 5.1 x 3.8 x 1.3 cm
Blue Peruvian opal drusy, Swarovski crystal,
seed beads; bead embroidery, stringing
PHOTO BY ARTIST

SUE HORINE
Mij's Dream ■ 2011
55 x 9 cm
Porcelain otter, glass cabochon,
seed beads, gemstone beads
PHOTO BY ARTIST

ANN TEVEPAUGH MITCHELL
Cook Inlet, Alaska ■ 2006
30 x 20 x 1 cm
Seed beads, thread, ostrich shell; peyote

DEBBIE ZOLLO
Lucrezia Necklace ■ 2011

33 x 14 x 0.6 cm
Labradorite cabochons, Japanese seed beads, Czech seed
beads, pearls, Czech glass cabochons; bead embroidery
PHOTOS BY DENNIS JOURDAN

JEANNIE BENCH
Her Song in the Night ■ 2011

1.3 x 2 x 38.1 cm
Suede, carved bone, gemstones, ammonites,
carved wooden beads, glass beads, brass clasp
PHOTO BY JESSICA STEPHENS

JENNIFER VANBENSCHOTEN
Lady in the Lake ■ 2006

Centerpiece: 14 x 12.5 cm
Handmade ceramic face, freshwater pearls, seed beads,
pressed glass beads; bead embroidery, spiral rope, peyote
PHOTOS BY SHERWOOD LAKE PHOTOGRAPHY

125

JEAN POWER
Geometric Beaded Beads ■ 2009

Each: 3 x 3 x 3 cm
Seed beads, wooden bead; peyote
PHOTO BY ARTIST

ANGELICA FAJA-BUSCHMANN
Vienna Bubbles ■ 2009

42 cm long
Japanese seed beads; bead crochet
PHOTO BY ARTIST

HELENA TANG-LIM
The Muse ■ 2009

62.5 cm long
Seed beads, porcelain beads, crystals; peyote
PHOTO BY ERIC LIM

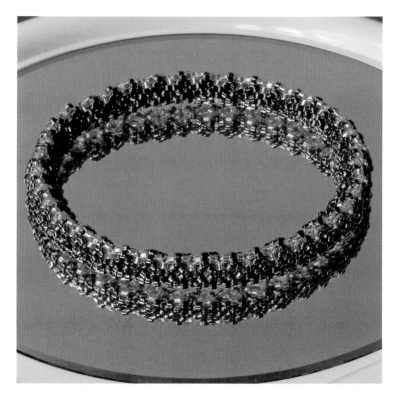

CAROL DEAN SHARPE
Between the Lines
Right-Angle Weave Cuff ■ 2010

4.5 x 21 cm
Seed beads, fishing line;
right-angle weave
PHOTO BY ARTIST

GERLINDE LENZ
Three Metals Triangular Bangle ■ 2010

7.5 x 7.5 x 0.8 cm
Bronze, cylinder beads;
extended right-angle weave
PHOTO BY ARTIST

MARCIE A. ABNEY
La Catedral Beadwoven Bangles ■ 2011

Each: 1.5 x 7.5 x 1.5 cm
Seed beads, Czech glass;
right-angle weave, peyote
PHOTO BY ARTIST

LINDSAY WISECUP
Stairway to Heaven ■ 2011

16 x 1 x 1 cm
Seed beads; Russian spiral, fringe
PHOTO BY LEILA CRANFORD

SUSAN LUTZ KENYON
Hooked on a Spiral ■ 1999
49 x 2 x 1.5 cm
Seed beads, wooden rondelles, clay bead, button;
bead crochet, right-angle weave, bead embroidery
PHOTOS BY TOM VAN EYNDE

LUCIE VEILLEUX
Caterpillar Bracelet ■ 2010

4.8 x 7 x 7 cm
Handmade wood components, glass beads,
elastic cord; cut, drilled, polished, threaded
PHOTO BY ARTIST

BRONWYNN LUSTED
Untitled ■ 2011

53 x 10 x 1 cm
Black ebony, white ebony, tagua
nut beads, waxed linen thread
PHOTO BY ARTIST

131

MARGO C. FIELD
Imperial Garden Necklace and Earrings ■ 2008
Necklace: 23 x 17 x 1.5 cm; earrings: 7.5 x 2 x 1 cm each
Seed beads, rivoli beads, glass beads; peyote, fringe, netting
PHOTOS BY PAT BERRETT

KIMBERLY STATHIS

Look with a View (Kaleidoscope Adventure) ■ 2011

Kaleidoscope: 5.1 cm long
Seed beads, Swarovski crystals and pearls;
off-loom beadweaving, peyote, spiral herringbone
PHOTO BY MARTIN KONOPACKI

CAROL S. TANENBAUM

Purple Multi-Strand Necklace ■ 2009

72 x 4.5 cm
African trade beads; strung
PHOTO BY GEORGE POST

133

MARCIE STONE
Visions of the Reef ■ 2011

19 x 16.5 x 1.3 cm
Vintage turquoise buttons, coral, turquoise,
pearls, seed beads; sculptural peyote
PHOTO BY GREG HANSON

FRANCIE BROADIE
Bough to Mother Nature ■ 2010
38 x 28 x 3.5 cm
Seed beads, lampworked beads, wire,
fabric, wire armature; peyote
PHOTOS BY STEPHEN CONWAY

135

YAEL KRAKOWSKI
Balloon Necklace ■ 2004

18 cm in diameter
Glass beads, cotton thread, brass; crochet
PHOTO BY ARTIST

MAYRA NIEVES-BEKELE
Jupiter's Moons ■ 2011
35 x 25 x 2 cm
Seed beads, crystals, amethyst; right-angle weave,
three-drop peyote, freeform netting
PHOTOS BY GEORGE POST

SUSAN MATYCH-HAGER
Fiesta Redux Necklace ■ 2010

23 x 20 x 6 cm
Handmade lampworked beads, crystals, pears, grosgrain
ribbon, wire, cotton; knotted, stitched, wire crochet
PHOTO BY ARTIST

REGINA DAIZEI BEAHM
Necklace Coral Reef ■ 2011

46 cm
Seed beads, Swarovski crystals, sponge
coral, turquoise chips, lampworked
twist cane, string-ons, dots
PHOTO BY GRACE C. BEAHM

LILLIAN BENRUBI
September ■ 2011

Dimensions unknown
Soda-lime glass, sterling-silver
findings, sterling-silver chain
PHOTO BY GREG KING

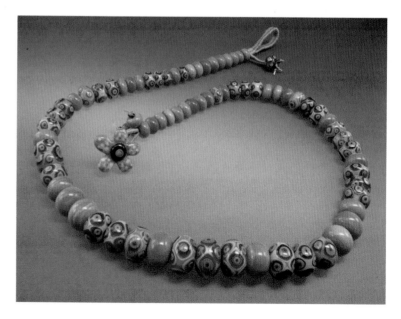

MANUELA WUTSCHKE
Claire de Lune ■ 2010

80 cm long
Soft glass, sterling silver, nylon
thread; woven, flameworked
PHOTO BY ARTIST

HARTMUT WUTSCHKE
It Takes Two to Tango ■ 2011

58 cm long
Lampworked beads, nylon thread
PHOTO BY MANUELA WUTSCHKE

LESLIE FRAZIER
Crystal Galaxy Beads ■ 2009

Largest bead: 25 x 25 x 25 cm
Seed beads, crystals, faux pearls, gold-filled
beads; right-angle weave, embellishment
PHOTO BY TOM FRAZIER

CARMEN ANDERSON
Evening Rainbow ■ 2010

81.3 cm long
Seed beads, Czech beads,
polymer clay; bead crochet
PHOTO BY ROBERT DIAMANTE

CARMEN ANDERSON
Circus Bling ■ 2008

63.5 cm long
Polymer clay, rubber
PHOTO BY ROBERT DIAMANTE

KATHARINA EDER
Fadenspiel Rainbow Necklace ■ 2011

16 x 1 x 47 cm
Antique seed beads, polyamide thread; bead crochet
PHOTO BY SIMONE ANDRESS

143

PATRICIA ZABRESKI
Spring Leaves ■ 2009
50.8 x 2.5 x 1.3 cm
Handmade lampworked glass beads, lampworked
etched spacer beads, Swarovski crystals
PHOTO BY JERRY ANTHONY

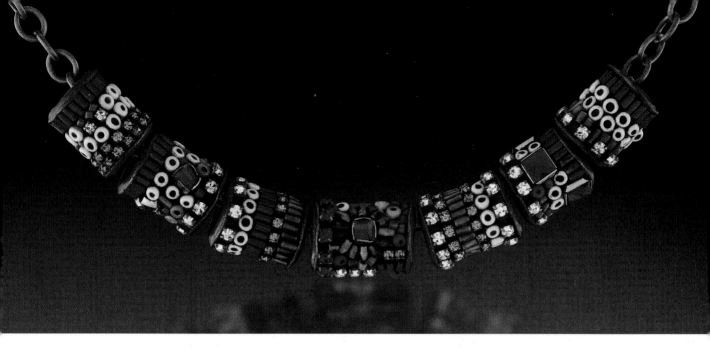

BETSY YOUNGQUIST
Copper Tube Bead Necklace ■ 2011
1.3 x 10 x 1.3 cm
Seed beads, coral beads, turquoise beads, vintage
glass stones, bugle beads, vintage glass beads,
copper pipe; hand worked, mosaic
PHOTO BY LARRY SANDERS

BETSY YOUNGQUIST
Copper Tube Bead Pendants ■ 2011
Each: 6.4 x 1.9 x 1.9 cm
Seed beads, coral beads, turquoise beads, antique
glass beads, brass beads, bugle beads, vintage glass
stones, copper pipe; hand worked, mosaic
PHOTO BY LARRY SANDERS

145

CARY FRANKLIN GASPAR
Great Balls ■ 2008

63.5 x 5.1 x 3.8 cm
Seed beads, turquoise discs, glass discs, pearls,
sterling silver; freeform right-angle weave
PHOTO BY TOM VAN EYNDE

FACING PAGE
KRISTIN KRAUSKOPF
Cleopatra's Scarab ■ 2011

Pendant: 6.3 x 4.4 cm
Seed beads, turquoise,
semiprecious stone beads,
metal beetle; bead embroidery
PHOTO BY CHRISTOPHER BURKE STUDIOS LLC

BETH BLANKENSHIP
Tidepool Pins/Necklace ■ 2010

Various dimensions
Seed beads, suede-like fabric;
bead embroidery, picot
PHOTO BY JESSICA STEPHENS

BETH BLANKENSHIP
Tidepool Bracelet ■ 2009
20.3 x 5.1 cm
Seed beads, suede-like fabric; bead embroidery, picot
PHOTOS BY JESSICA STEPHENS

NOME MAY

Garden Collection ■ 2007

Dragonfly: 5 x 5 x 0.5 cm
Antique seed beads, pearls, gemstones,
gold, silver; bead embroidery
PHOTO BY MARTIN KILMER

SANDY LENT
Bevy of Butterflies ■ 2010
7.6 x 40.6 x 0.6 cm
Acid-etched lampworked butterflies, seed beads
PHOTO BY RYDER GLEDHILL

MARCY ANTLE
Southwest Princess ■ 2010
25 x 18 x 3 cm
Seed beads, stones, pearls, turquoise chips; embroidery
PHOTO BY LISA BARTH

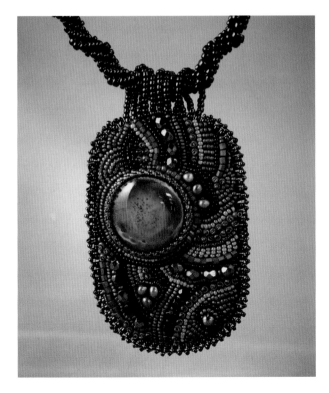

CAMILLE SIMMONS
Sea Dreams Pendant ■ 2009
7 x 5 x 0.5 cm
Lampworked cabochon, seed beads,
freshwater pearls; bead embroidery
PHOTO BY ROBERT B. SIMMONS

DOT LEWALLEN
Garden Buzz ■ 2010
5.1 x 20.3 x 1.3 cm
Resin-encased insect, seed beads, pearls,
sequins; bead embroidery, peyote
PHOTO BY CHRIS LEWALLEN

LEAH COMERFORD
Estuary ■ 2010
43.2 x 12.7 x 1.6 cm
Seed beads, dichroic glass, jasper, cubic zirconia, turquoise,
Swarovski crystals, bugle beads, mother-of-pearl birds,
suede-like fabric; bead embroidery, peyote, fringe, picot edging
PHOTOS BY ADAM DESIO

Showcase 500
beaded jewelry

LAURIE DANCH
Belvedere Jasper Bracelet ■ 2009

2 x 17.5 x 1.3 cm
Belvedere jasper cabochons, seed beads, crystals,
pearls; bead embroidery, peyote, right-angle weave
PHOTOS BY MARTIN KONOPACKI

155

TATYANA FEDORIKHINA
Under the Sea Necklace ■ 2011

61 cm long
Fan coral, prehnite, pearls, amethyst, seed beads, silk,
silver wire; micro macramé, Russian spiral, brick
PHOTOS BY JENNIFER PARKER

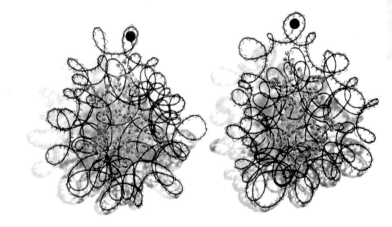

D'ELIN LOHR
Dawn Mist ■ 2010

102 cm long
Seed beads, Czech glass, assorted beads,
lampworked beads; bead crochet
LAMPWORKED BEADS BY JENNY FRISKE BAER
PHOTO BY ARTIST

DORIS BETZ
Earrings ■ 2006

Each: 5.5 x 3.5 x 0.4 cm
Glass beads, iron wire, acrylic
PHOTO BY ARTIST

MARGIE DEEB
Veil ■ 2006

20 x 10.5 cm
Seed beads, costume coins; loom weaving
LOOMWORK BY FRIEDA BATES
PHOTO BY JOHN HAIGWOOD

BETTY STEPHAN
Butterfly Dreams ■ 2011

33 x 25 cm
Butterfly wings, acrylic sheets, glass
beads, seed beads, glass cabochons;
bead embroidery, beadweaving
PHOTO BY TIM FUSS/PIXELWAVE

159

EVE ALTA EDMONDS
Skunk ■ 2009
16.5 x 1.3 cm
Millefiori beads, Venetian glass, sterling-silver
wire, wax cotton cord; wire wrapping
PHOTO BY MARTIN BARKER

ANITA SPENCER
Tribal Necklace ■ 2010
48 x 2.5 x 1.3 cm
Soda-lime glass, onyx, silver clasp, silver
leaf, gold leaf, powdered glass enamel
PHOTO BY JERRY ANTHONY

SUSAN TERESE MCKECHNIE
Garnish ■ 2009

Various dimensions
Electroplated kale and acorn, Swarovski rivolis and
crystals, seed beads; chevron, peyote, fringe, netting
PHOTO BY TOM VAN EYNDE

LAURIE NESSEL
My Dreams ■ 2010

Various dimensions
Handmade glass bead, seed beads,
Swarovski crystals; herringbone
PHOTO BY MARK HENDRICKSON

163

KERRY D. VINE
Under the Tuscan Sun ■ 2010

42.5 x 5 x 1 cm
Seed beads, glass cabochons;
freeform netting, freeform peyote
CABOCHONS BY ANDREA WEIR
PHOTO BY TOM HASSLER

ARBUMILLIA FLORIFEROUS
River of Life ■ 2008

26 x 15 x 2 cm
Seed beads, bugle beads, Venetian beads,
tiger's-eye chips, carnelian; Ndebele,
peyote, brick, moss technique
PHOTO BY ARTIST

ELIZABETH RUSNELL
Milagros ■ 2010

41 x 5.5 x 3.5 cm
Handmade polymer beads, seed beads, glass
beads; strung, wirework, fringe, embellishment
PHOTO BY JOE JUSTAD

MELANIE L. DOERMAN
Adele, the Can-Can Girl ■ 2011

59 x 6 x 2.5 cm
Seed beads, crystals, porcelain, brass, glass,
fiber; peyote, netting, spiral rope
PHOTO BY ARTIST

167

VICTORIA HENSON
Champagne Wishes ■ 2011

4 x 18.4 x 0.7 cm
Seed beads, amber, Champagne cap, Swarovski crystals,
suede, gold-filled clasp; peyote, right-angle weave
PHOTOS BY JOE MANFREDINI

VICTORIA HENSON
Peek-a-Boo ■ 2011
5.7 x 19.7 x 0.5 cm
Photo, resin, Bakelite, brass screw heads, labradorite, vintage sew-on,
hematite, seed beads, drop beads, leather; bead embroidery, peyote
PHOTOS BY JOE MANFREDINI

MARY DIMATTEO
Multi-Strand Bead-Embroidered Necklace ■ 2010
Pendant: 14 x 6.5 cm; necklace: 61 cm long
Agate cabochon, pearls, seed beads, gold charlottes, gold
cones, gold beads, vermeil clasp; bead embroidery, spiral rope
PHOTO BY ROBERT DIAMANTE

MARY DIMATTEO
Gifts of the Sea Necklace ■ 2011

75.8 cm long
Pearls, pink crystals, seed beads, silver cubes,
sterling-silver findings; kumihimo braiding
PHOTO BY ROBERT DIAMANTE

171

JULIE LONG GALLEGOS
Klimt Cuff ■ 2010

18.5 x 6 cm
Seed beads, freshwater pearls; loomwork

ANA GARCIA
Copper Channel Bracelet ■ 2008
1.3 x 19 cm
Seed beads, Czech glass beads, copper beads; right-angle weave
PHOTOS BY JOSEPH NASKAR

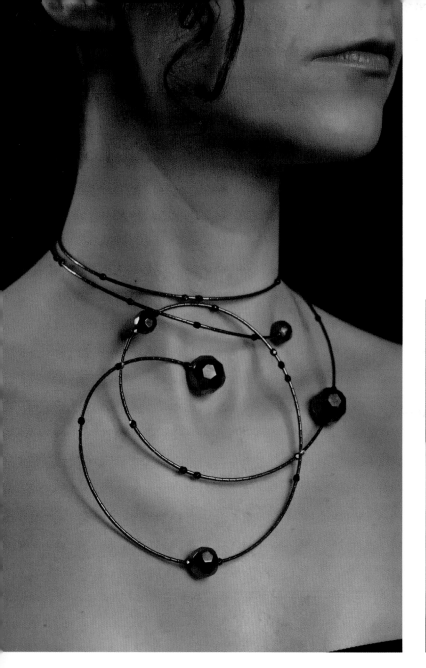
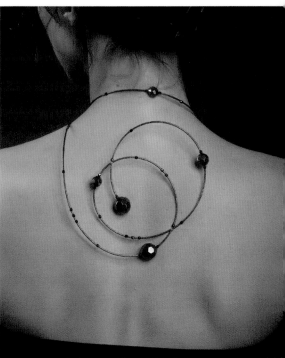

JULIA DUSMAN
Milonga ■ 2010
19 x 13 x 1.5 cm
Fire-polished glass beads, memory wire
PHOTOS BY JENS LOOK

Showcase 500
beaded jewelry

KYUNGHEE KIM
Salvia ... Salvia ■ 2010
35 cm long
Silver, wooden beads
PHOTO BY KWANGCHUN PARK

HEIDI KUMMLI
Black Forest ■ 2010
30.5 x 20.3 x 2.5 cm
Seed beads, cabochons, bone deer; bead embroidery

HEIDI KUMMLI
Bite Me ■ 2011

15.2 x 10.2 x 1.3 cm
Seed beads, cabochons, bone bear, ermine tails,
silver spoon handle; bead embroidery
PHOTOS BY ARTIST

LARKIN JEAN VAN HORN
Soaring Raven ■ 2009
50 x 22 x 1 cm
Seed beads, bugle beads, porcelain raven, fused-glass cabochons,
bone feathers, crystals, pressed glass; bead embroidery
PORCELAIN RAVEN BY LAURA MEARS
PHOTO BY G. ARMOUR VAN HORN

LARKIN JEAN VAN HORN
Bon Odori ■ 2010

43 x 22 x 1 cm
Seed beads, fused-glass cabochons,
pressed glass; bead embroidery
PHOTOS BY G. ARMOUR VAN HORN

179

KAREN BACHMANN
Sputnik Earrings ■ 2011

Each: 5.5 x 1.8 x 1.8 cm
Acrylic, sterling silver; carved,
sandblasted, inlaid
PHOTO BY RALPH GABRINER

DHARMESH KOTHARI
NAMRATA KOTHARI
Lantern Charm Bracelet ■ 2007

2.5 x 20.5 x 2.8 cm
Rock crystal, rubellites, 18-karat yellow gold
PHOTO BY KEVIN CHUNG

KERRY D. VINE
Raise a Glass ■ 2006
47 x 8.8 x 1 cm
Found beach glass, crystal, freshwater pearls, seed
beads; peyote stitch, spiral rope, surface embellishment
PHOTO BY TOM HASSLER

181

LILIANA CÎRSTEA GLENN
Pennaceous ■ 2010
8.5 x 24 x 9 cm
Sterling-silver wire, chain, and beads, lampworked
glass beads, seed beads, elastic string

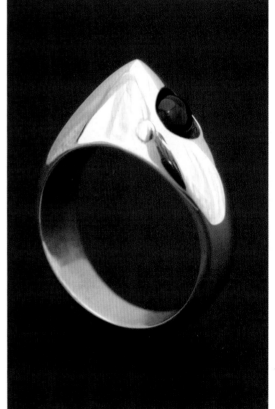

MELANIE SMITH
Anticlastic Beaded Bangle ■ 2002

3.5 x 3.5 cm
Sterling silver, fine silver, seed beads; hand forged
PHOTO BY ARTIST

LUCIE VEILLEUX
A Sort of Fish ■ 2011

2.3 x 1.8 x 0.7 cm
Sterling silver, amethyst beads, sterling-silver
wire, wax; carved, cast, polished, riveted
PHOTO BY ARTIST

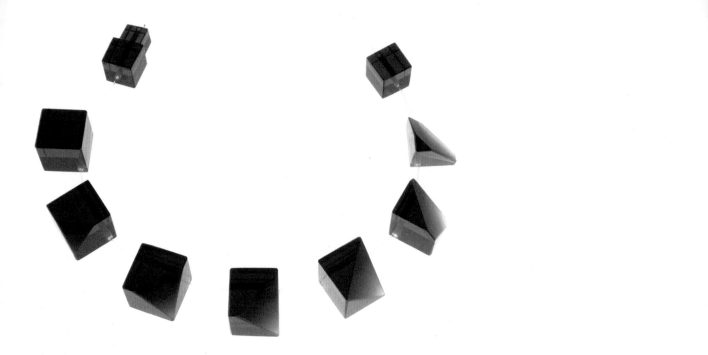

CHIARA ANTONIETTI
Cube Disappearing ■ 2010

22 cm long
Nylon, crystal beads; fused, ground
PHOTO BY MAURIZIO ELIA

CAMILLE ARGEANAS
Mosaic Pendant ■ 2011

6 x 3 cm
Brass wire, turquoise chip
beads; wire wrapping
PHOTO BY SAMANTHA TRUJILLO

BIANCA EDMONDS
Summer Pods Necklace ■ 2011

17 x 12.5 cm
Glazed porcelain, seed beads,
metal heishi beads, sterling silver;
hand formed, crimp and wire
PHOTO BY MARTIN BARKER

185

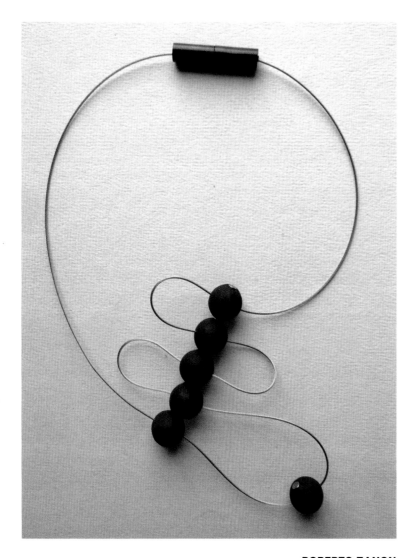

ROBERTO ZANON
Quasi Sette ■ 2007
28 x 24 x 1.5 cm
Rubber beads, cadmium magnets, steel wire, plastic
PHOTO BY ARTIST

ANTJE STOLZ
Rip-Off ■ 2010
30 x 30 x 3 cm
Hematite beads, plastic, graphite powder
PHOTO BY ARTIST

TOP
DORIS BETZ
Brooch ■ 2004
8 x 6.5 x 1.5 cm
Glass beads, copper, red gold
PHOTO BY ARTIST

BOTTOM
DORIS BETZ
Brooch ■ 2006
4 x 4 x 4.5 cm
Glass beads, silver
PHOTO BY ARTIST

CHEQUITA NAHAR
Switi Watra Brooch ■ 2010
11 x 14 x 2.8 cm
Porcelain beads, pinewood beads,
cord, silver, snakewood
PHOTO BY GALLERY MARZEE

187

IRINA ASTRATENKO
Inspiration Choker ■ 2010
34 x 13 x 9.5 cm
Seed beads, beads, threads, wool, chain; tatting, felting
PHOTO BY ARTIST

REBECCA R. STARRY
Shooting Stars Brooches ■ 2011

Largest: 10.7 x 10.7 x 1.5 cm
Seed beads, accent beads, shurikens, assorted findings;
right-angle weave, off-loom stitches
PHOTO BY JESSICA STEPHENS

JUAN RIUSECH DE HARO
Solar-System Necklace ■ 2010

18 x 8 cm
Glass beads, liquid-gold enamel inlay,
white agate, silver; fabricated
PHOTO BY SEBASTIEN JOLY

TAMUNA LEZHAVA
Georgian Autumn ■ 2010
44 x 3 cm
Seed beads, Swarovski beads and crystals,
artificial pearls, metal-covered beads,
velvet ribbon; peyote, tubular Ndebele

SUZANNE GOLDEN
Red Flowers ■ 2010

5 x 15 cm
Acrylic beads, seed beads; tubular, spiral peyote
PHOTO BY ROBERT DIAMANTE

DEBBIE ZOLLO
Hohokam Honey Bracelet ■ 2011
40.6 x 8.9 x 0.6 cm
Lapis-lazuli cabochons, pewter face beads, vintage seed beads,
Japanese seed beads, button clasp; bead embroidery, peyote, stringing
PHOTOS BY DENNIS JOURDAN

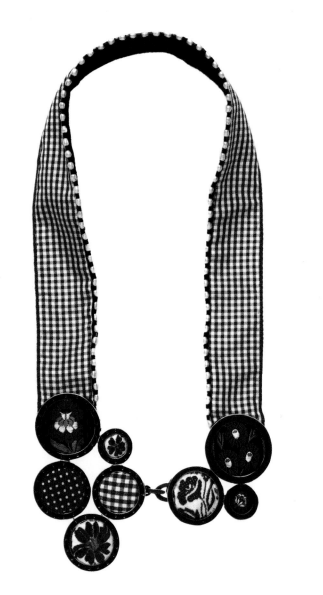

INGEBORG VANDAMME
Looking for Mr. Right ■ 2010
Each: 20 x 20 x 2.5 cm
Anodized aluminum, silver, glass beads, pearls,
textiles, textile beads; sewn, hand fabricated
PHOTOS BY ARTIST

REBECCA MCKAY
Pink, Paper, and Metal ■ 2011

43 x 1 x 1 cm
Paper-rolled beads, silver-plated
pendant, chain, wire; looped
PHOTO BY ARTIST

195

MARCIA LAGING-CUMMINGS
Jailbreak ■ 2010
36 x 14.5 x 3.5 cm
Seed beads, crystals, accent beads;
right-angle weave, peyote, brick, square
PHOTO BY ROGER BRUHN

JULIE LONG GALLEGOS
Coral Snake Lariat ■ 2011
183 x 10 x 30 cm
Seed beads, agate beads, onyx beads,
glass beads; Ndebele, stringing
PHOTO BY GEORGE POST

PATTY HABERMAN
Attack ■ 2011
48 x 22 x 3 cm
Felt beads, crystals; machine stitching,
hand stitching, spherical pentagon
PHOTOS BY DAVID ORR

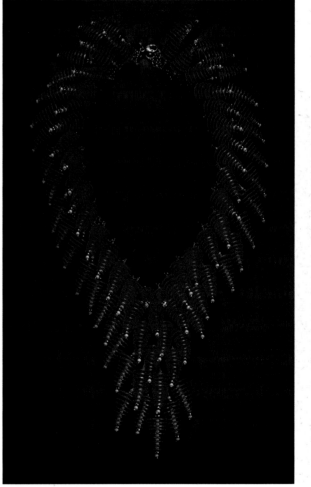

INGER MARIE BERG
Red Cone Necklace ■ 2009

48.5 cm long
Sterling silver, plastic, hematite,
glass beads; hand fabricated
PHOTOS BY JAN ERIK LANGHES

MARCIA DECOSTER
Party Girl ■ 2010
56 x 17 x 3 cm
Seed beads, crystals; right-angle weave
GLASS BY HEATHER TRIMLETT
PHOTO BY ARTIST

MARCIA DECOSTER
Kongming Lantern ■ 2011
10 x 5 x 4 cm
Seed beads, crystal, felt; beadweaving
PHOTO BY ARTIST

BARBARA SCOTT-FISHER
Mosaic Bracelets ■ 2011

Each: 45 x 180 cm
Glass beads, seed beads, carnelian, carved agate, coral,
tiger's-eye, turquoise, smoky quartz, copper, pearls; freeform
PHOTO BY RALPH GABRINER

JEANNETTE COOK
Bead Party Necklace ■ 2004
75 x 10 x 2 cm
Seed beads, niobium wire, fumed glass beads,
Venetian blown-glass beads, furnace glass beads
PHOTOS BY MARCIA DECOSTER

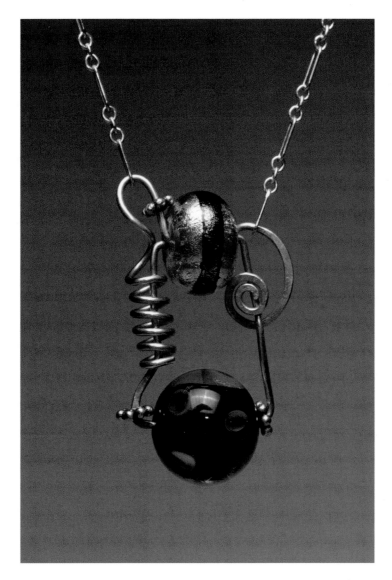

CANDACE CLOUD MCLEAN
My Birthday Beads ■ 2007

Pendant: 4.2 cm long
Handmade glass beads,
sterling-silver beads; wirework
PHOTO BY BRIAN JAMES

SUSAN MATYCH-HAGER
Summer Crayon Box Necklace ■ 2011
23 x 16 x 2 cm
Handmade lampworked beads, silver,
seed beads, wire; stringing, wirework
PHOTO BY ARTIST

SUSAN RIDGWAY
Dump Friendly ■ 2008

45.7 x 22.9 cm
Toy lizards and frog, vintage sugar beads, German vintage
glass, leaf glass, seed beads; freeform netting

BEKI HALEY
Enchanted ■ 2011
Pendant: 6 x 8 x 1.5 cm
Seed beads, crystals, fringe beads; peyote, netting,
branched fringe, braided herringbone
PHOTO BY SHAWN HALEY

STEPHANIE SERSICH
Warm Colors Necklace ■ 2010
65 cm long
Handmade glass beads, handmade
glass button, seed beads; stringing
PHOTO BY TOM EICHLER

KELLY J. ANGELEY
Links and Threads ■ 2009
50.8 x 17.8 x 1.9 cm
Seed beads, glass button, brass bead caps;
peyote, brick, herringbone, spiral rope
PHOTO BY BARRY JENSEN

MARGIE DEEB
Serpentine Loops ■ 2011
30 x 18 cm
Czech faceted beads, glass seed
beads; right-angle weave
PHOTO BY ARTIST

JENNIFER SHIBONA
Life's a Carnival ■ 2010
39 x 11.5 x 6.5 cm
Copper leaf, ceramic face, wire, seed beads, glass
beads; peyote, square, Russian spiral, brick, netting
PHOTO BY EILEEN DITULLIO

Showcase 500
beaded jewelry

LAUREN BUCHAN
Eyes of the Forest ■ 2011

30 x 9 x 4 cm
Seed beads, stones, boro beads,
taxidermy eyes, spikes, pearls; embroidery,
herringbone, peyote, flamework
PHOTO BY ARTIST

ANNETA VALIOUS
Song of the Rain ■ 2011
28 x 12 x 2 cm
Charoite, pearls, rhinestone chains, soutache braid,
metal chains, seed beads; soutache embroidery
PHOTOS BY ARTIST

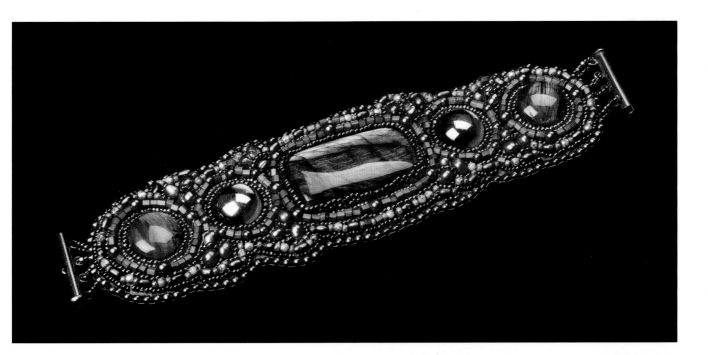

DEBBIE ZOLLO
Lucrezia Bracelet ■ 2011

21 x 5.1 x 0.6 cm
Labradorite cabochons, Czech glass cabochons, Czech
seed beads, Japanese seed beads; bead embroidery
PHOTOS BY DENNIS JOURDAN

SUSAN RIDGWAY
Millsie's Brooch ■ 2011
38.1 x 17.8 cm
Felt, leather, vintage brooch, cabochons,
seed beads, sequins, crystals; bead embroidery
PHOTO BY LAMPING PHOTOGRAPHY

RACHEL WEISS
Sunset Stone Necklace ■ 2010

48.2 cm wide
Laguna agate, lace agate,
pearls; bead embroidery
PHOTO BY LARRY SANDERS

NANCY DALE
Regency ■ 2011
45.7 cm long
Seed beads, Swarovski chatons, drops, and crystals,
Namibian pietersite cabochons; bead embroidery,
herringbone, right-angle weave, peyote, fringe
PHOTO BY SHERWOOD LAKE PHOTOGRAHY

DIXIE GABRIC
I Dream of Egypt ■ 2009

15 x 16.5 cm
Metal pharaoh, brass scarabs, seed beads;
peyote, backstitch, bead embroidery
PHOTO BY JEFF GABRIC

TONI RATNER MILLER
Serenity ■ 2010

26 cm long
Seed beads, labradorite, glass, Peruvian opal, jasper, abalone,
blue opal, amazonite, glass, crystal beads, suede-like fabric;
peyote, spiral, Cellini spiral, bead embroidery
PHOTO BY GEORGE POST

CANDICE ST. JACQUES
Picasso Triptych Statement Necklace ■ 2010

45 x 11.3 x 1.3 cm
Picasso jasper cabochons, labradorite chips,
Czech faceted beads, seed beads; peyote
PHOTOS BY EDDY ANTHONY

217

MARCIE STONE
Southwest-Spirit Necklace ■ 2011
19 x 16 x 1.3 cm
Glass buttons, vintage Native American
buttons, seed beads; peyote
PHOTO BY GREG HANSON

MET INNMON
Crystal Triad Necklace ■ 2009
28 x 5.5 x 1.8 cm
Cylinder beads, seed beads, crystals; peyote,
herringbone, kudu spiral variation
PHOTOS BY LARRY HANSEN

CHRISTINE MARIE NOGUERE
Andromeda ■ 2004
20 x 38 x 2.5 cm
Japanese glass seed beads, rubber O-rings;
off-loom weaving, right-angle weave
PHOTO BY PHIL POPE

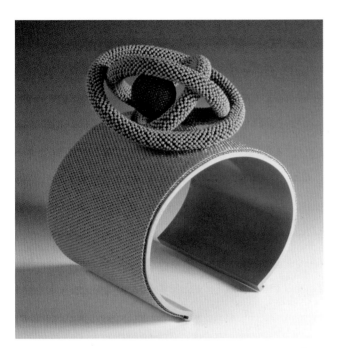

CHRISTINE MARIE NOGUERE
Titania (Jewelry for Giants, No. 5) ■ 2007

23 x 19 x 15 cm
Japanese glass cylinder and seed beads, cork ball,
butyl cord, maple wood, pearlescent paints;
right-angle weave, peyote, bent, laminated, painted
PHOTOS BY PHIL POPE

CHRISTINE MARIE NOGUERE
Arc to Arcturus (Jewelry for Giants, No. 6) ■ 2011

23 x 19 x 15 cm
Japanese glass cylinder and seed beads, cork ball,
butyl cord, maple wood, pearlescent paints;
right-angle weave, peyote, bent, laminated, painted
PHOTOS BY PHIL POPE

MARCIE A. ABNEY
The Queen's Crown Beadwoven Bracelet ■ 2011

20 x 2.5 x 2.5 cm
Seed beads, Czech glass; beadweaving
PHOTO BY ARTIST

SANDY TALLY
Sky-Blue Waters ■ 2009

3.8 x 22.2 cm
Seed beads, bugle beads, pearls, rhinestones,
larimar, suede-like fabric, brass blank;
bead embroidery, moss, peyote
PHOTO BY BRIAN HUTSON

MELANIE T. ROBBINS
The Peacock Nebula ■ 2010
20 x 13 cm
Seed beads, fringe beads, trim beads; freeform Ndebele
PHOTO BY STORYBOARDLIFE.COM

ELEANOR LUX
Another Important Collection ■ 2010
9 x 16 cm
Washers, O-rings, aluminum wrapped loops
PHOTOS BY CINDY MOMCHILOU

Showcase 500
beaded jewelry

SARA SALLY LAGRAND
Cecilia Brooch ■ 2011

17.8 x 10.2 x 15.9 cm
Lampworked glass beads, steel wire,
copper wire, polymer clay
PHOTO BY ARTIST

NANCY CAIN
Crystal Tile Ring ■ 2010

3.6 x 3.2 cm
Seed beads, cylinder beads,
crystals; circular peyote, flat peyote,
stringing, embellishment
PHOTO BY DAVE WOLVERTON

225

MARTHA WILKES
ELIZABETH LYNE
Surface Progression over a Linnenbrink ■ 2011

46 x 20 x 2.5 cm
Effetre glass lampworked beads, brass, silver
PHOTO BY JASON DOWDLE

JESSICA KAPLAN LUNDEVALL
Retro Seascape Bracelet ■ 2005

20 x 4 x 2 cm
Seed beads, glass beads, vintage glass; peyote
PHOTOS BY SYNDI SIMON

KAREN J. LAUSENG
Sewing Snap Necklace ■ 2010
46 cm long
Sewing snaps, sterling-jump rings
PHOTO BY ARTIST

JUAN RIUSECH DE HARO
Necklace/Crown ■ 2006

10 x 30 cm
Hair beads; tension set
PHOTOS BY SEBASTIEN JOLY

LANA MAY
Amethyst Sunset ■ 2011

Necklace: 40 x 3 cm; bracelet: 19 x 4 cm
Swarovski pearls, Delica beads, glass drops,
antique button, seed beads; embellishment
PHOTOS BY MARK HENDRICKSON

MYRA E. SCHWARTZ
Equus ■ 2006
66 x 3.8 x 2.5 cm
Antique Meerschaum cheroot holder, antique butterscotch amber, lampworked glass, raku, antique glass,
antique turquoise, new turquoise, antique coral, serpentine, sterling silver, seed beads; strung, knotted

JEANNETTE COOK
Parasol Earrings ■ 2010
Each: 4 x 3 x 3 cm
Silk, armature, glass beads, Swarovski crystals
PHOTO BY MELINDA HOLDEN

YAEL KRAKOWSKI
Desert Flower Necklace ■ 2008

36 cm long
Oxidized silver, carnelian beads,
thread, silver pieces; crochet
PHOTOS BY ARTIST

ARIANNE VAN DER GAAG
Untitled ■ 2007

20 cm long
Antique beads, diamonds; strung
PHOTO BY RENS HORN

SABINE LIPPERT
Crownie Pendant ▪ 2011

3.8 cm in diameter
Chatons, crystal beads, pearls, seed beads
PHOTOS BY ARTIST

237

MARY ANN HELMOND
Art Nouveau Peacock ■ 2011
Bracelet: 4 x 21 cm; necklace: 66 x 11 cm; earrings: 5.5 x 2 cm each; ring: 2.3 x 2.6 cm
Seed beads, lampworked beads, wire, sterling-silver findings;
brick, peyote, tubular herringbone, St. Petersburg stitch
PHOTOS BY ROXANN BLAZETCH-OZOLS (COLLABORATION)

VALERIE LB KUZMA
Art-Deco Feathered Collar ■ 2010
17.8 x 34.3 cm
Seed beads, crystals, peacock feathers,
suede-like backing; bead embroidery, peyote
PHOTOS BY JOSEPH NASKAR

239

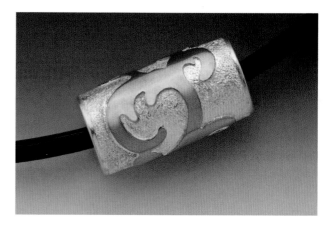

NANCY MELI WALKER
Bellissimo Chased Bead ■ 2011

14 x 13 x 1.5 cm
22-karat gold bead, 22-karat gold
clasp, pearls, silk; chased, fabricated,
sewn, kumihimo braiding
PHOTO BY STAN SHOLIK

KATHLEEN E. WADE
Textured Cylinder Bead ■ 2011

1.9 x 1 cm
22-karat gold, Argentium sterling silver,
steel cable; fabricated, fused, textured
PHOTO BY GEORGE POST

MADDALENA ROCCO
Nyx Necklace ■ 2011

28 x 28 cm
Pearl, beaded onyx, horn, silver, onyx
mosaic, silver engraving of Burin
PHOTOS BY ARTIST

FAITH WICKEY
Bright Leaf Necklace ■ 2010

45 cm long
Lampworked glass beads, crystals; strung
PHOTO BY LARRY SANDERS

JEAN CAMPBELL
Peyote Buttons ■ 2009

46 cm long
Seed beads, leather, sterling
silver findings; peyote
PHOTO BY ARTIST

243

SIS MORRIS
Vespertilio ■ 2011
13.5 x 22.5 x 1.5 cm
Ceramic focal bead, seed bead, bat charms; embroidery
PHOTO BY AUDREY SECHLUR AND SARA BREUSS

Showcase 500
beaded jewelry

MELISSA INGRAM
Melbournian: A Couture Neckpiece ■ 2011
48 x 8 x 3 cm
Seed beads, cylinder beads, magatamas, crystallized Swarovski elements,
vintage Swarovski chatons, Japanese vintage micro-glass pearls,
magnetic clasp; right-angle weave, peyote, freeform sewing, herringbone
PHOTO BY TWK STUDIOS

LISA KAN
Cascading Blooms ■ 2010
45.7 x 33.7 x 2.5 cm
Seed beads, crystals, pearls, Czech glass,
lampworked glass antique beads; twisted
tubular herringbone, peyote
PHOTO BY ARTIST

PAM KILLINGSWORTH
Bella Vintagio ■ 2011

Various dimensions
Lampworked cabochons and beads, seed beads, pearls, crystals,
satin cord; bead embroidery, kumihimo braiding, stringing
PHOTO BY ARTIST

MARSHA WIEST-HINES
Raindrops on Lilacs ■ 2011
13 x 7 x 46 cm
Seed beads, cylinder beads; herringbone, peyote,
triangle weave, netting, fringe, stringing
PHOTO BY ARTIST

247

JAMIE CLOUD EAKIN
Santa Fe Sky ■ 2011
27.9 x 17.8 cm
Boulder opals, kyanite, drusy, red tiger's-eye,
sunset jasper, freshwater pearls, seed beads, copper
tube beads, metal drops; bead embroidery
PHOTO BY ARTIST

JERI LAMBERT
Dancing in the Desert ■ 2011
8.5 x 5.7 x 1.1 cm
Crystal, seed beads, Tila beads, pearl drops,
leather strap; bead embroidery, peyote
PHOTO BY PICTURE PERFECT PHOTOGRAPHY

LEE WILKINS
Sunset in Montana ■ 2010

6.4 x 5.1 cm
Montana agate cabochon, tiger's-eye beads, Swarovski crystals, seed beads; bead embroidery, stringing
PHOTO BY ARTIST

JEAN CAMPBELL
Star of India ■ 2006

Pendant: 6 cm diameter
Seed beads, crystals, pressed glass, gold; peyote, fringe
PHOTO BY MARGIE DEEB

ARBUMILLIA FLORIFEROUS
Moonlight Sonata ▥ 2010

46 x 16 x 3 cm
Seed beads, crystals, acrylic glass bead, black
agate; peyote, Ndebele, brick, 3D-flower
technique, moss technique, embellishment
PHOTO BY ARTIST

MELISSA GRAKOWSKY
Cultivation ■ 2010

40.6 x 20.3 x 5 cm
Polymer clay, pearls, seed beads,
nonwoven base, leather; bead embroidery
PHOTO BY ARTIST

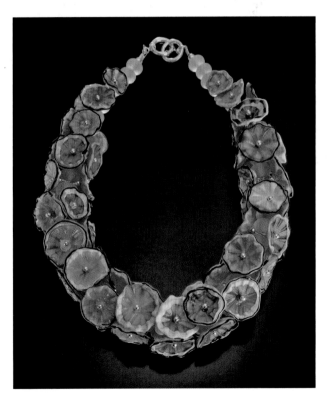

JULIA BEHRENDS
Black Necklace **and** *Hot Black Necklace* ■ 2011

Each: 42.5 cm long
Black diamond faceted round beads, black Tahitian pearls, gray Tahitian pearls, golden South Sea pearls, white cultured freshwater pearls, 18-karat yellow gold beads, pink tourmaline cabochon, round brilliant diamond; strung, fabricated

SANDY LENT
Limpets ■ 2008
3.8 x 40.7 x 3.8 cm
Lampworked glass discs, sterling-silver rounds, acid-etched lampworked beads; wired

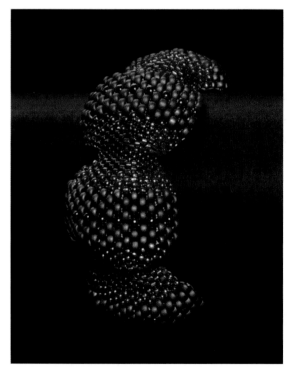

SHARRI MOROSHOK
Colors of Winter ■ 2010
46 cm long
Seed beads, smoky quartz, sterling silver; peyote
PHOTO BY ARTIST

LAINY ABBOTT
It's Gonna Be a Bumpy Ride ■ 2011
20.5 x 3 cm
Seed beads; peyote
PHOTO BY ARTIST

MAGGIE MEISTER
Olivia ■ 2010

15.2 x 19.1 x 1.3 cm
Seed beads, freshwater pearls;
right-angle weave, peyote
PHOTO BY GEORGE POST

JOHANNA ZITTO
Collare Ondulato Necklace ■ 2011

43 cm long
Seed beads, silver toggle; tubular peyote

JOHANNA ZITTO
Dew Drops on Moss Necklace ■ 2011
51 cm long
Metallic-finish magatamas,
jasper beads; netting
PHOTO BY BARBARA MCDONOUGH

VERONICA JONSSON
The Eye of the Flower ■ 2011
17 x 6 cm
Acrylic eye, crystals, pearls, seed beads, fake
leather, leather, aluminum; bead embroidery
PHOTO BY MIKAEL HOLLSTEN

YVETTE RASHAWN ESTIME
On the Fringe ■ 2010
15.2 x 60.9 cm
Seed beads; Russian fringe,
right-angle weave
PHOTOS BY SHAYMAMIN

VALERIE BROWN
Mysterious Twilight ■ 2009

50 cm long
Seed beads, pearls, mother-of-pearl beads,
Swarovski pearls, lantern beads; tubular
herringbone, right-angle weave, fringe
PHOTO BY PAUL AMBTMAN

JANICE BERKEBILE
North Shore ■ 2008

80 x 35 x 1 cm
Puka shell, cone shell, silver shell beads,
silver chain, silver clasp; wirework
PHOTO BY ARTIST

ÉVA DOBOS
Kahleen Bracelet ▪ 2011

2.5 cm, 8.8 cm in diameter
Seed beads, Delica beads, drops, fire-
polished donuts, crystal bicones, pressed
beads, imitation pearls; embellishment
PHOTO BY SANDOR BODOGAN

SABINE LIPPERT
Baroque Dimensional Bracelet ▪ 2009

2.5 x 21.6 cm
Firepolished beads, seed beads,
drop beads, crystal beads
PHOTO BY ARTIST

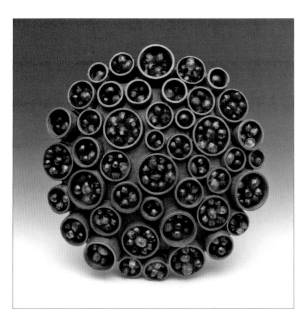

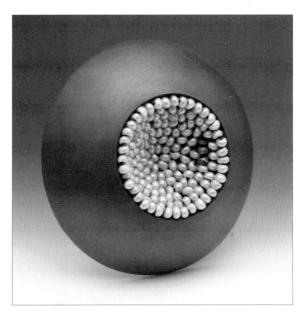

TOP LEFT
BOLINE STRAND
Seed Pod Brooch ■ 2011

5.3 x 5.4 x 1.3 cm
Sterling silver, ruby, amethyst, tourmaline,
garnet beads; fabricated, oxidized, beaded
PHOTO BY GEORGE POST

BOLINE STRAND
Inner Life Brooch ■ 2009

4.6 x 4.6 x 1.7 cm
Sterling silver, seed pearls, 18-karat gold
beads; fabricated, oxidized, beaded
PHOTO BY GEORGE POST

TOP RIGHT
BOLINE STRAND
Seed Capsule Brooch ■ 2011

4.7 x 4.7 x 1.4 cm
Sterling silver, amethyst, sapphire, tourmaline,
garnet beads; fabricated, oxidized, beaded
PHOTO BY GEORGE POST

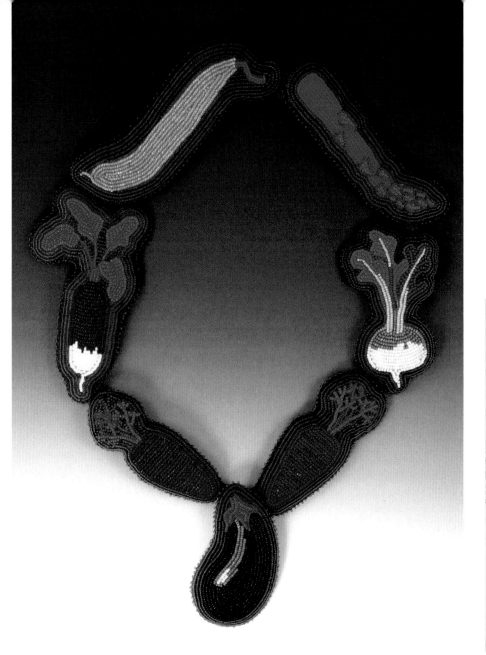

BETH BLANKENSHIP
Ode to the Vegetable Pins/Necklace ■ 2007

Various dimensions
Seed beads, suede-like fabric;
bead embroidery, picot
PHOTOS BY JESSICA STEPHENS

ANN TEVEPAUGH MITCHELL
Teapots ■ 2005
30 x 20 x 1.5 cm
Seed beads, thread; right-angle weave
PHOTO BY DEAN POWELL

CHRISTY PUETZ
How to Disappear Completely ■ 2010
24 x 18 cm
Seed beads; peyote
PHOTO BY DAVE SAKER

LISA KAN
Serenity ■ 2010
45.7 x 17.8 x 1.3 cm
Seed beads, pearls, lampworked
glass, crystal rivoli; spiral peyote,
circular herringbone
PHOTO BY ARTIST

PAULETTE BARON
Circles and Spirals ■ 2010
25 x 13 x 2 cm
Seed beads, Swarovski crystals and pearls; peyote
PHOTO BY CARRIE JOHNSON

AIJA KIVI
Necklace 02 ■ 2011

28 x 34 cm
Silver, freshwater pearls, textile
PHOTO BY LEMBIT JÜRGENSON

JENNIFER WELLS
Line Cuffs ■ 2011

Various dimensions
Seed beads, felt, aluminum,
canvas, pearls; bead
embroidery, edging
PHOTO BY ARTIST

NANCY CAIN
Crystal Bridges ■ 2009

Each: 2 x 2.5 x 2 cm
Seed beads, cylinder beads, crystals,
crystal pearls; circular peyote, flat
peyote, embellishment, stringing
PHOTO BY DAVE WOLVERTON

I-SHAN TSAI
Peacock Feathers ■ 2004
Each: 55 x 16 x 0.5 cm
Metal parts, seed beads, steel wire; right-angle weave
PHOTO BY DANNY TSAI

MARGO C. FIELD
Water Lily Necklace and Earrings ■ 2009

Necklace: 21 x 14 x 2.5 cm; earrings: 10 x 2 x 1 cm each
Seed beads, wire armature, pewter clasp; herringbone, peyote, fringe
PHOTOS BY PAT BERRETT

CAROLE HORN
Wildweeds Necklace ■ 2010

22.9 x 16.5 cm
Seed beads; herringbone, peyote
PHOTO BY D. JAMES DEE

HUIB PETERSEN
Pansy ■ 2010

40 cm long
Seed beads; peyote
PHOTO BY ARTIST

LYNSEY BROOKS
Pandora ■ 2011
25 x 15 x 2 cm
Seed beads, fine polished glass
beads, crystals, glass drops, drusy
quartz; bead embroidery, peyote
PHOTO BY BENJAMIN PARKER

CATHARINA THOMAS
Coco's Cuff ■ 2011
6 x 7.5 x 4.5 cm
Seed beads, cabochons,
semiprecious stones; bead embroidery
PHOTO BY ARTIST

SARA SALLY LAGRAND
ROBIN YOUNG

Monster ■ 2005

88.9 x 5.1 cm
Lampworked glass beads, shells,
crystals, seed beads; freeform stitch
PHOTO BY ARTIST

ISOLINA PEREZ
Open-Heart Necklace ■ 2008

Pendant: 10.5 x 7 x 0.5 cm
Freshwater pearls, sterling-silver
wire, sterling-silver chain; forged
wirework, weaving, wire wrapping
PHOTO BY PETER CLOUGH

YVONNE CABALONA
Mineral Magic ■ 2009

Pendant: 5.1 x 4.5 x 1.3 cm
Hematite cabochon, mineral cabochon,
peach moonstone, Czech glass, seed
beads; bead embroidery, stringing
PHOTOS BY ARTIST

DIANE HYDE
Wisconsin Memories 1952 ■ 2010

35.6 cm long
Seed beads, crystal bicones, glass pearls, old photo, vintage watch parts, old keychain,
glass bottle, charms, stampings, suede-like material; bead embroidery, stringing
PHOTOS BY ARTIST

275

JEAN POWER
Geometric 3-4-1 ■ 2007

11.5 x 11.5 x 2.5 cm
Cylinder beads; peyote
PHOTO BY ARTIST

LAURA MCCABE
Wonderstone Spiked Cuff ■ 2010

18 x 4.5 x 2 cm
Custom-cut wonderstone points, glass seed beads,
crystal beads, 14-karat gold clasp; peyote, embellishment
PHOTO BY MELINDA HOLDEN

CAROL DEAN SHARPE
Golden Blooming-Bead Peyote Pendant ■ 2011

2.5 x 4.3 cm
Cylinder beads, fishing line; peyote
PHOTO BY ARTIST

CAROL DEAN SHARPE
Ribbed Peyote Cuff ■ 2011

5 x 21.5 cm
Seed beads, fishing line; embellished peyote
PHOTO BY ARTIST

MARY HICKLIN
Midnight Passage Necklace ■ 2009

53 cm long
Seed beads, crazy lace agate, sterling-silver
setting, pearls; gourd, bezel fabricated
AGATE CUT BY LEIGH BECKER
PHOTO BY BARRY BLAU

CHRISTINE GUIBARA
Pearl Watercast Necklace ■ 2010

75 cm long
Freshwater pearls, silk string, argentium sterling
silver, 14-karat gold; water casting, hand knotting
PHOTO BY ARTIST

Showcase 500
beaded jewelry

LESLEE FRUMIN

Crystal Elements Bracelets ■ 2009

Each: 18.6 x 1.7 x 1.7 cm
Swarovski crystals and pearls, Japanese
seed beads; netting, peyote, brick
PHOTO BY HAP SAKWA

279

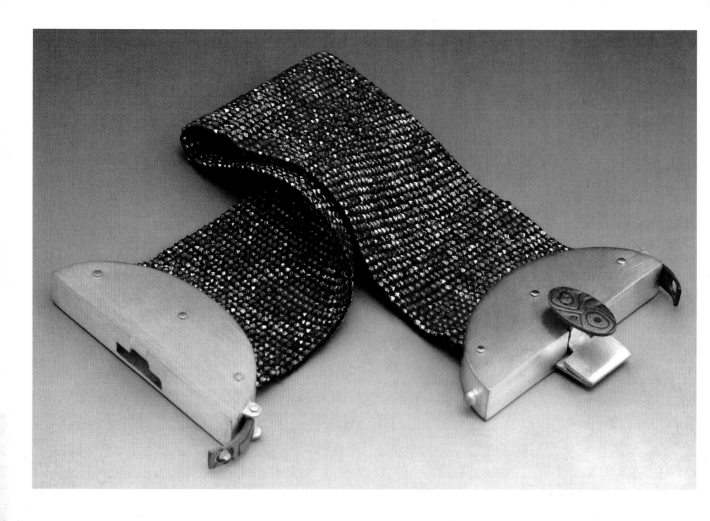

L. SUE SZABO
Ripple ■ 2010

16.5 x 4.2 x 0.6 cm
Sterling silver, mokume gane of copper and nickel, vintage metal
beads, metals, silk thread; hand fabricated, riveted, on-loom beading
PHOTO BY ERICA CRISSMAN

LAURIE DANCH
Bronze Leaf Cuff ■ 2011
2.5 x 21.3 x 1.3 cm
Vintage brass elements, pearls, seed beads, crystals;
bead embroidery, peyote, right-angle weave

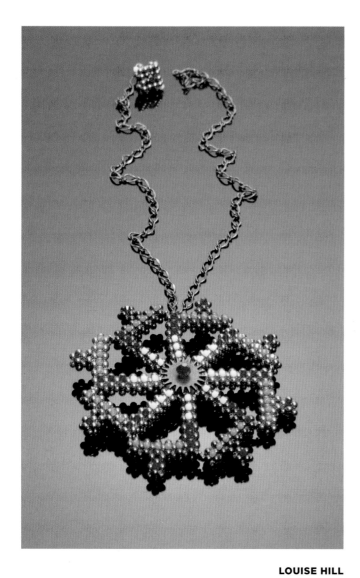

LOUISE HILL
Pinwheel Pendant ■ 2011
36 x 9 x 1.5 cm
Swarovski pearls and crystals, brass
gear, brass chain; right-angle weave
PHOTO BY ARTIST

MEGHAN PATRICE RILEY
Medusozoa Earrings ■ 2011
Each: 15.2 x 3.8 x 3.8 cm
Copper, sterling silver, nylon-coated steel,
copper beads; hand fabricated, strung
PHOTO BY TOKY PHOTOGRAPHY

INGEBORG VANDAMME
Red Coral Necklace ▪ 2006
23 x 23 x 1.5 cm
Coral beads, paper, paraffin, felt
PHOTO BY ARTIST

HARTMUT WUTSCHKE
Raindrops ■ 2011

47 x 1.2 x 0.6 cm
Lampworked beads, nylon thread
PHOTO BY MANUELA WUTSCHKE

KAREN J. LAUSENG
Paper Clip Necklace ■ 2010

48 cm long
Paper clips, glass beads, sterling jump rings
PHOTO BY ARTIST

DEBRA EVANS-PAIGE
Sunrise on Sand ■ 2006
50.5 x 5.9 x 0.5 cm
Porcelain, sterling silver, silk; hand formed,
textured, oxidation fired, hammered, knotted
PHOTO BY DANIEL DINSMORE

ANITA SPENCER
Of Egg, Pod, Stone, and Twig ■ 2009
48 x 4 x 2 cm
Soda-lime glass, Precious Metal Clay, sterling-silver spacer
beads, lampworked glass beads, twigs, cork; molded
PHOTO BY JERRY ANTHONY

LAURA DEAKIN
Confused Earrings ■ 2010

54 cm long
Sterling-silver earring studs,
polyester resin, pigment; oxidized
PHOTOS BY ARTIST

KAREN BACHMANN
Burnt Balls Necklace ■ 2011

49 cm long
Maple wood, onyx, sterling silver;
carved pyrography, strung
PHOTO BY RALPH GABRINER

MIKKI FERRUGIARO
Urchin Collar ■ 2010
39 x 5.2 x 2.5 cm
Rivoli beads, seed beads; peyote
PHOTOS BY ARTIST

JENNIFER WELLS
Ripple ■ 2011
8.5 x 5 x 5.5 cm
Seed beads, pearl, felt, aluminum,
leather; bead embroidery, edging
PHOTO BY ARTIST

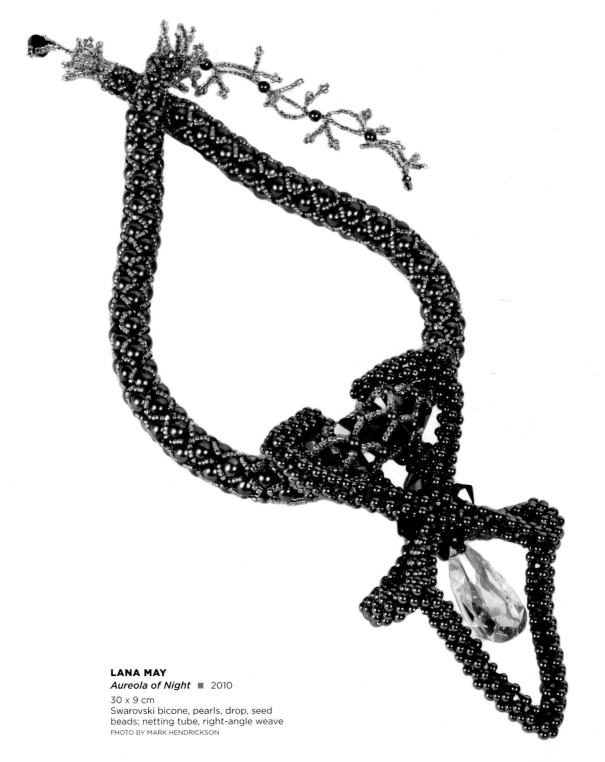

LANA MAY
Aureola of Night ■ 2010

30 x 9 cm
Swarovski bicone, pearls, drop, seed
beads; netting tube, right-angle weave
PHOTO BY MARK HENDRICKSON

LINDA EDEIKEN
Blue Cielito ■ 2011
41 x 6.4 cm
Seed beads, turquoise,
sterling silver, onyx, pearls
PHOTO BY MELINDA HOLDEN

LOIS SIMON ROSENTHAL
Arrowhead Ribbon Necklace ■ 2011
32 x 4.5 x 1 cm
Cylinder seed beads, thread; braided
PHOTO BY ROBIN MILNE

VICTORIA HENSON
Tribal Sophistication ■ 2011

44.5 x 7.6 x 0.7 cm
Seed beads, cylinder beads, charlotte beads, daggers, labradorite, turquoise, metal
beads, Swarovski crystals, pearls, suede-like fabric; peyote, right-angle weave
PHOTO BY JOE MANFREDINI

291

REBECCA ZIMMERMANN
Seeds of Gold ■ 2004
18 x 16 x 2.5 cm
Chinese lantern tree seeds, 23-karat
gold leaf, embroidery thread
PHOTOS BY ARTIST

HELENA TANG-LIM
Nefertiti ■ 2011

Largest pendant: 6 x 5 cm
Seed beads, Tila beads, crystals, magatamas,
pressed glass; right-angle weave, Ndebele
PHOTO BY ERIC LIM

293

VALERIE LB KUZMA
Royalty Necklace ■ 2011
24.1 x 15.2 cm
Seed beads, crystals, vintage pearls,
enameled shells, faceted beads, jasper
cabochon; bead embroidery, peyote
PHOTO BY JOSEPH NASKAR

CARMEN ANDERSON
Konjo Fikir (Beautiful Love) ■ 2005

91.4 cm long
Polymer clay, brass, hemp, cowrie shell,
kekeore shell, Ethiopian engagement pendant
PHOTO BY ROBERT DIAMANTE

JOSEPH NASKAR
Copper Corrupted ■ 2011

2.2 x 3.2 x 3.2 cm
Hollow copper beads, solid copper ring
shanks; tubular even-count peyote
PHOTO BY ARTIST

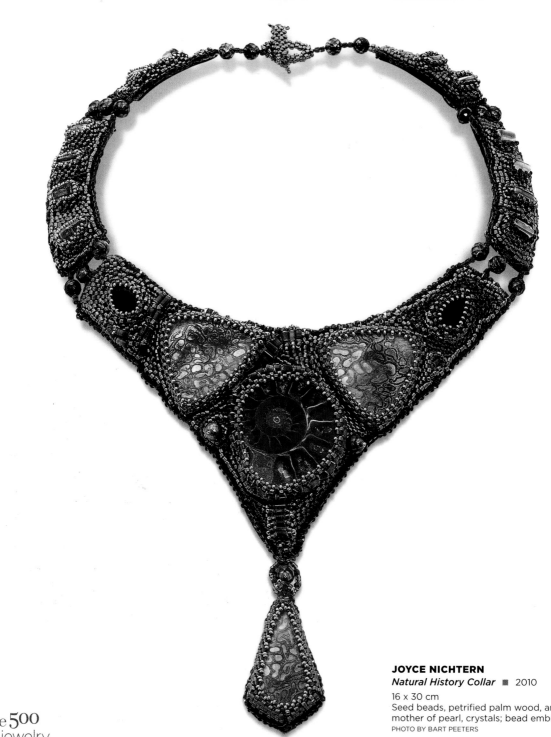

JOYCE NICHTERN
Natural History Collar ■ 2010

16 x 30 cm
Seed beads, petrified palm wood, ammonite,
mother of pearl, crystals; bead embroidery
PHOTO BY BART PEETERS

SYLVIE CAMPS
Timucua Cuff—Dedicated to the Florida Indian Tribe ■ 2010

19.5 x 6 x 1 cm
Seed beads, accent beads, tiger's-eye; freeform peyote
PHOTO BY DAVID CAMPS

COOKY SCHOCK
Butterfly Brooch ■ 2010

10.2 x 8 x 1.6 cm
Brass, gourd, copper wire, glass beads, metal beads,
rivets; fold formed, etched, woven, connected, riveted
PHOTO BY JOSEPH NASKAR

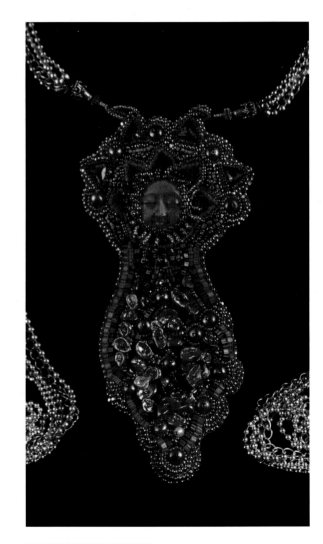

JOCELYN COOLEY
Offering ■ 2010
110 cm long
Seed beads, silver clay; Dutch
spiral, hand formed, imprinted
PHOTO BY BRUCE SHIPPEE

DARCY WYNNE ROSNER
Mardi-Gras Queen: Lariat ■ 2010
83 x 7 x 1 cm
Seed beads, vintage crystals, keishi pearls, freshwater pearls,
bone, leather, sterling silver; bead embroidery, fringing, peyote
PHOTO BY ROBERT LIZOTTE

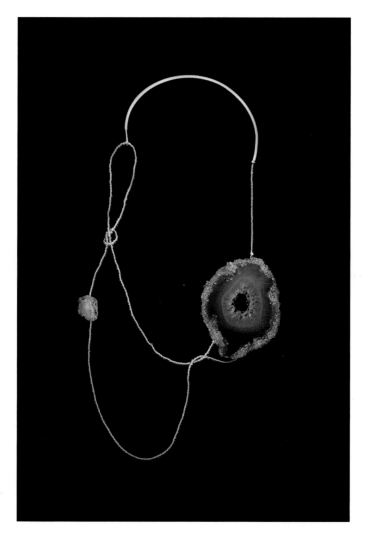

ANTJE STOLZ
Bubbly Agate ■ 2007
30 x 12 x 1 cm
Rock crystal beads, glass beads,
agate, silver, plastic material
PHOTO BY SALLY KISS AND JULIA ISRAEL

EVELYN LETFUSS
Tech Ears ■ 2009
Each: 2 x 1.5 x 0.8 cm
Circuit board parts, glass cubes,
glass leaves; freeform peyote
PHOTO BY HAP SAKWA

TERESA SHELTON
Stryke Out ■ 2010
2.5 x 22.5 x 0.5 cm
Printed circuit board, seed beads,
bead cap; peyote stitch
PHOTO BY ARTIST

EVELYN LETFUSS
Gertrud's First Computer ■ 2009

30 x 8 x 0.5 cm
Circuit board and other computer parts, millefiori glass beads,
pearls, sand-polished crystals, seed beads; freeform peyote
PHOTO BY HAP SAKWA

LINDA EDEIKEN
Bengal Beauty ■ 2011
41 x 6.4 cm
Seed beads, rubies, sapphires, champagne
citrine, pearls; off-loom freeform peyote
PHOTO BY MELINDA HOLDEN

HUIB PETERSEN
Blue Waterlilies ■ 2008

50 cm long
Seed beads, bugle beads;
peyote, triangular weave
PHOTO BY ARTIST

SHER BERMAN
Autumn Lariat ■ 2009

106.7 cm long
Lampworked glass beads, bone, Japanese
glass seed beads, soda-lime glass, enamel
powders, stringers; bead crochet rope
PHOTO BY TOM VAN EYNDE

JOHN K. ARCHER
Charmed ■ 2011
32 x 150 x 150 cm
Steel, enamel paint; welded
PHOTO BY ELIZABETH TORGERSON-LAMARK

NINA OWENS
Lock-and-Key Necklace ■ 2010
40.6 x 7.6 cm
Glass beads, seed beads, metal
components; freeform peyote
PHOTO BY PURE RED

305

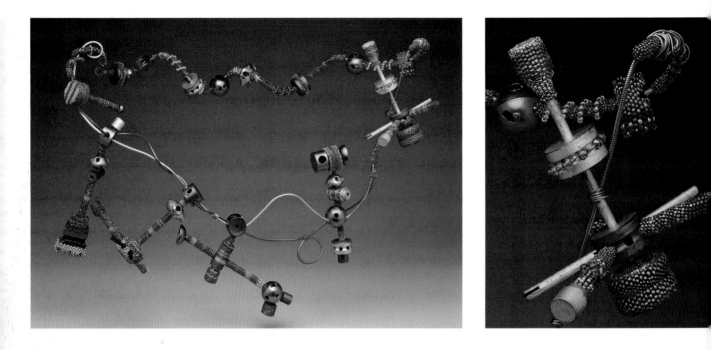

TONI RATNER MILLER
Constellation Collar ■ 2011

45.7 cm wide
Mini construction toys, seed beads, glass beads, sterling-silver beads, gold-tone chain and beads, plumber's solders, paint pens; flat peyote, spiral peyote, wirework

AMY KATZ
Bottle Cap Bling ■ 2010

2.8 x 1.3 x 0.5 cm
Seed beads, crystals, bottle-cap bead; peyote
PHOTO BY CARRIE JOHNSON

CHENG-SYUAN LIU
When You Assume That I Had Only One Posture ■ 2011

5 x 5 x 5 cm
Brass, fishing line; right-angle weave
PHOTOS BY ARTIST

WARREN FELD
Little Tapestries: Ghindia ■ 2011
15 x 13 x 0.5 cm
Seed beads, Delica beads, crystals, brass beads,
brass chain, brass clasp; ladder, square, quilling
PHOTO BY ARTIST

MARCIE A. ABNEY
Tumbling Tilas Beadwoven Bangles ■ 2011
Each: 1.5 x 7 x 1.5 cm
Seed beads, Tila beads; peyote
PHOTO BY ARTIST

MELANIE L. DOERMAN
Dreamscape ■ 2010

6.5 x 19 x 2 cm
Seed beads, crystals; peyote
PHOTO BY ARTIST

ANA GARCIA
Peyote and Pyrite ■ 2010

1.3 x 16.5 cm
Seed beads, pyrite, Czech glass beads; peyote
PHOTO BY JOSEPH NASKAR

MELISSA INGRAM
Magic Carpet Ride Cuff ■ 2011

5 x 20 cm
Seed beads, vintage Swarovski crystal chatons, crystallized Swarovski
elements, magnetic clasp; right-angle weave, peyote, herringbone
PHOTOS BY TWK STUDIOS

BETH BLANKENSHIP
Seashell Bracelet ■ 2007

18 x 6 cm
Seed beads, suede-like fabric; bead embroidery, picot
PHOTO BY JESSICA STEPHENS

313

CARY FRANKLIN GASPAR
In One End ■ 2007
2.5 x 20.3 x 1.3 cm
Seed beads, 14-karat gold beads, pearls,
sterling-silver beads, sterling-silver
rings, metal snap; freeform Ndebele
PHOTO BY TOM VAN EYNDE

SHERRY SERAFINI
Domestic Goddess ■ 2011
60.9 cm long
Seed beads, cabochons, brushes,
chains; bead embroidery
PHOTO BY ARTIST

LESLIE ROGALSKI
Tribal Cuff ■ 2011

15 x 5 x 1.5 cm
Japanese Tila beads, glass round beads,
freshwater pearl nuggets, bone rondelles;
modified flat right-angle weave, embellishment
PHOTO BY ARTIST

LESLIE ROGALSKI
Steampunk Herringbone Cuff ■ 2010

16 x 3.5 x 2 cm
Cylinder beads, chain links, watch parts,
jump rings, rubber O-rings; herringbone
PHOTO BY ARTIST

CAMILLE ARGEANAS
Egyptian Mosaic Bracelet ■ 2010
22 x 3 cm
Seed beads, button, brass wire; wire wrapping
PHOTOS BY SAMANTHA TRUJILLO

KERRIE SLADE
Maid Marian's Quiver ■ 2009
8 x 4 x 1.5 cm
Seed beads, cylinder beads, sterling-silver pin; brick
PHOTO BY ARTIST

RACHEL NELSON-SMITH
Beon Freo Necklace ■ 2011

23 x 16 x 2 cm
Glass, crystal, acrylic, nylon, sterling silver;
peyote, herringbone, right-angle weave
PHOTO BY ARTIST

317

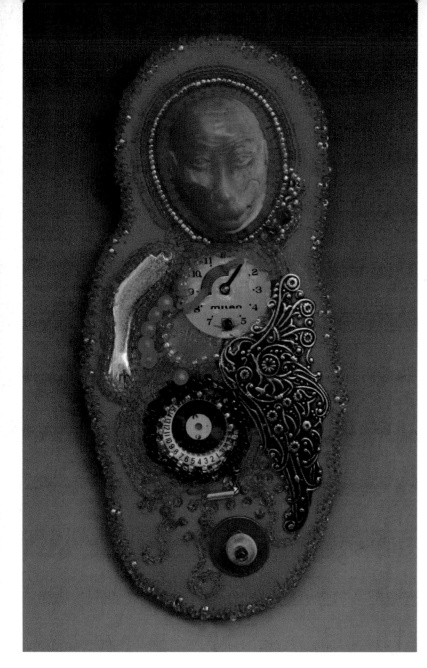

JEANNIE BENCH
The Monkey King – Brooch ■ 2010
10.2 x 7.6 cm
Suede, found objects, brass stampings,
resin, metal charms, seed beads
PHOTOS BY JESSICA STEPHENS

SUSAN TERESE MCKECHNIE
Feeling Punky ■ 2011
Various dimensions
Polymer clay, brass findings, seed
beads, bone beads; peyote, edging
POLYMER CLAY FACE BY GAIL BAKER
PHOTO BY TOM VAN EYNDE

FAITH WICKEY
Bright Flower Necklace ■ 2010
45 cm long
Lampworked glass beads, crystals; strung
PHOTO BY LARRY SANDERS

ANN TRISTAN
ANITA TRISTAN

Heavenly Pearls Multi-Strand Necklace ■ 2011

20.3 x 21.6 cm
Cultured pearls
PHOTO BY SUSAN MATYCH-HAGER

KATHARINA EDER
Fadenspiel ■ 2010

50 cm long
Antique seed beads, polyamide
thread; bead crochet
PHOTO BY SIMONE ANDRESS

MARCIA LAGING-CUMMINGS
Goldilocks Sings the Blues ■ 2007
36 x 18 x 1 cm
Seed beads, resin beads, crystal drop, accent
beads; right-angle weave, peyote, square
PHOTO BY ROGER BRUHN

TANYA TEGMEYER-RODRIGUEZ
La Cage de Perles (The Beaded Cage) ■ 2011
28.5 cm long
Seed beads, Swarovski crystals, micro pearls,
crystals, glass beads, silk cord, crystal stone;
right-angle weave, netting, peyote
PHOTO BY DOUGLAS M. SALEWSKY

TONI RATNER MILLER
First Crocus ■ 2010
45.7 cm long
Seed beads, Swarovski crystals, amethyst, glass beads,
chalk turquoise, sterling-silver wire, wooden base beads,
handmade sterling-silver clasp; peyote, Cellini spiral
PHOTO BY GEORGE POST

MARSHA WIEST-HINES
Persephone's Return ■ 2010

37 cm long
Seed beads, cylinder beads, pearls, hand-painted lace,
sterling-silver findings; bead embroidery, stringing
PHOTO BY ARTIST

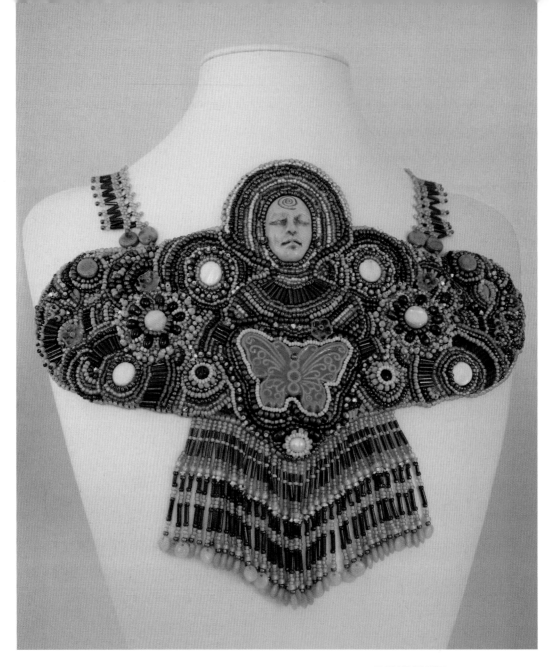

HOLLY KLINE
Transcendence ■ 2010

33 X 22.8 cm
Seed beads, pearls, turquoise, copper, Swarovski crystals,
rose gold, polymer clay; bead embroidery, netting
PHOTO BY ARTIST

SUE HORINE
Carnelian Garden ■ 2010

53.5 x 8.5 cm
Silver flowers, cabochons, seed beads,
glass beads, silver beads; bead embroidery
PHOTO BY ARTIST

TAMERA MICKELSON
Hard Wired ■ 2011
4 x 3.8 x 2 cm
Seed beads, craft wire, recycled computer
parts; right-angle weave, peyote
PHOTOS BY JELIZA PATTERSON

PAULETTE BARON
Autumnal Flora ■ 2011

36 cm long
Seed beads; right-angle weave, peyote
PHOTOS BY CARRIE JOHNSON

MYRA E. SCHWARTZ
Prima ■ 2011

71.1 x 5.1 x 3.8 cm
Antique ballerina pipe, lampworked glass, coated wire; strung
LAMPWORK BY MAUREEN HENRIQUES, PEGGY PRIELOZNY,
MARY JEAN MARTIN, MARY COBBLE, AND MARYANN LINDEN
PHOTO BY ARTIST

MARILYN L. MARTIN
Crayola Shake ■ 2009

45.7 cm long
Lampworked beads, leather cord,
Moretti Italian glass; fire torched
PHOTOS BY REBECCA A. ANDREW

ARBUMILLIA FLORIFEROUS
Land of Matissia ■ 2006
32 x 20 x 2 cm
Seed beads, bugle beads, tiger's-eye
chips; netting, peyote, brick, looping,
square, 3D-flower technique, paisleys
PHOTO BY ARTIST

DEB FAIRCHILD
Johanna's Reef ■ 2008

132 x 10 cm
Seed beads, shells; freeform right-angle weave
PHOTO BY SHEILA PERRY

JOHANNA ZITTO
Shoreline Finds Necklace ■ 2011

58 cm long
Seed beads, crackle-finish glass beads, clam shells, assorted daggers,
drop beads, vintage button clasp; freeform peyote, spiral rope
PHOTO BY BARBARA MCDONOUGH

MELANIE POTTER
Metamorphosis ■ 2011

25 x 25 x 6 cm
Seed beads, zircons, prongs, rose montees;
chevron chain, peyote, netting
PHOTO BY SCOTT POTTER

WENDY ELLSWORTH
Summer Passion ■ 2000

51.5 x 9.2 x 4.1 cm
Dichroic glass cabochon, dichroic lampworked beads,
seed beads, glass leaves, glass flowers, freshwater
pearls; freeform gourd, freeform herringbone
PHOTO BY DAVID ELLSWORTH

ANGELICA FAJA-BUSCHMANN
Kinko ■ 2011

2.5 x 19 x 0.5 cm
Seed beads, Czech glass beads; net
weaving, chevron, embellishment
PHOTO BY ARTIST

SHAYNA PRENTICE
Flaxen Plain ■ 2010
20 x 15 x 1 cm
Rock crystals, shells, fossil ivory, labradorite,
copper, glass; hand needlewoven, hand sewn
PHOTOS BY ARTIST

SHAYNA PRENTICE
A Winter's Branch ■ 2010

27 x 19 x 2 cm
Manzanita, pearls, coral, shells, metal
seed beads; hand needlewoven
PHOTO BY ARTIST

DHARMESH KOTHARI
NAMRATA KOTHARI
Mogul Tassel Pendants ■ 2008

Each: 50 x 1.5 x 4.5 cm
Tanzanite and rubellite, pomegranate spinel,
black spinel, 18-karat yellow gold
PHOTO BY KEVIN CHUNG

CYNTHIA MCEWEN
Shanghai Impressions Necklace ■ 2010
44 x 2.7 x 1.2 cm
Lampworked glass beads, seed beads,
ceramic beads, sterling silver
PHOTO BY STUDIO 37

CYNTHIA MCEWEN
Cinderella Night Gold Necklace ■ 2010
50 x 2.6 x 1.3 cm
Lampworked glass bead, glass beads,
copper beads, jasper, sterling silver
PHOTO BY STUDIO 37

EVELYN LETFUSS
Blackened Fish, BP-Style ■ 2010

31 x 16 x 1 cm
Seed beads, crystals, cylinder beads,
Spandex; freeform peyote, bead embroidery
PHOTO BY HAP SAKWA

PENNY ZOBEL
Reclamation ■ 2004
40 x 35 x 3.5 cm
Seed beads, cubes, leaves; right-angle weave, peyote
PHOTOS BY CHRIS AREND

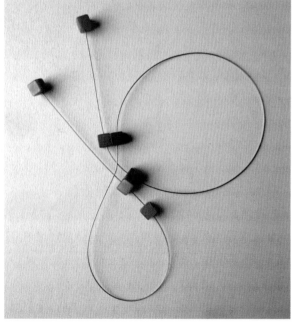

ROBERTO ZANON
Cubrescal ■ 2008

30 x 23 x 1 cm
Resin beads, cadmium
magnets, steel wire, plastic
PHOTO BY ARTIST

ALIKI STROUMPOULI
Fruit Necklace ■ 2008

35 x 15 x 4 cm
Plastic beads, glass beads, wood
beads, coral; bead embroidery
PHOTO BY ARTIST

ANNA BELOM
Tropical Waters Lariat ■ 2008

31.8 x 1.3 x 1 cm
Blue Peruvian opal, aquamarine, chrysoprase, prehnite,
quartz, apatite, tourmaline, sterling silver; wire wrapping
PHOTOS BY ARTIST

345

MARGIE DEEB
Holding the Hope ■ 2011
41 x 9 cm
Seed beads, acrylic glass, glass cabochons; embroidery, stringing
PHOTO BY ARTIST

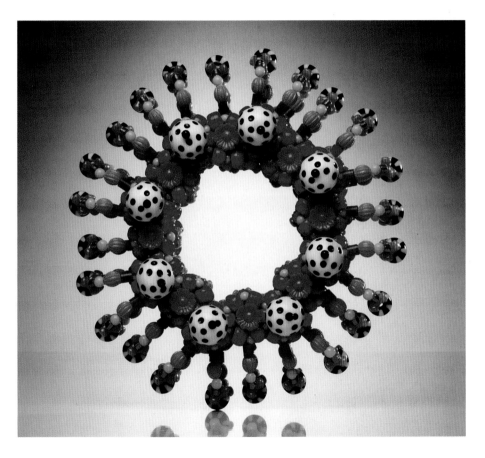

SUZANNE GOLDEN
Polka Dotty ■ 2011

7 x 16 cm
Acrylic beads, seed beads;
right-angle weave, embellishment
PHOTOS BY ROBERT DIAMANTE

REBECCA R. STARRY
Out of the Blue ■ 2008

5.7 x 20 x 1.4 cm
Seed beads, razor blades, snap
closure; right-angle weave
PHOTOS BY JESSICA STEPHENS

BARBARA SCOTT-FISHER
Octopus Bracelet ■ 2008

5 x 17.5 cm
Seed beads; freeform right-angle weave
PHOTO BY RALPH GABRINER

RUANN EWING
Shell Critter Pendant ■ 2011

9 x 4 x 3 cm
Seed beads, pearls, shell; tubular peyote
PHOTOS BY JOE WITTKOP

DONNA FROMHAGEN
Sanibel Shells Necklace and Earrings ■ 2008

Necklace: 27 x 10 x 1 cm; earrings: 2 x 2 x 1 cm each
Triangle seed beads, drops, shells; freeform peyote
PHOTO BY SYNTHIA SIMON

ELEANOR LUX
A Lizard Face-Off ■ 2010

4 x 12 cm
Seed beads, fabric, plastic pipe, kapok
stuffing; Yoruban beading techniques
PHOTOS BY CINDY MOMICHILOU

353

NOME MAY
Koi Pond Necklace ■ 2007
20 x 15 x 0.5 cm
Antique seed beads, gemstones,
silver; bead embroidery
PHOTO BY MARTIN KILMER

Showcase 500
beaded jewelry

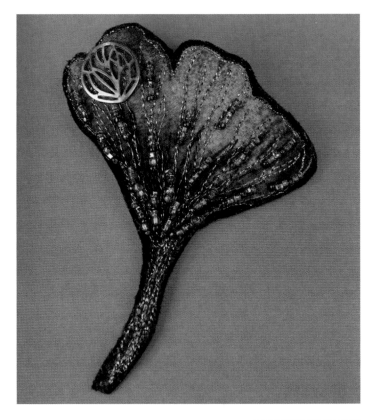

DARLENE HABANEK
SUSAN READING
Night Sky Gingko Fiber Art Pin ■ 2010
10 x 10.5 x 0.5 cm
Commercial cotton fabric, gold metallic thread,
seed beads, gold charm; painting, embellishment
PHOTO BY ARTISTS

PAMM HORBIT
Ammasso Ring ■ 2010
2.5 x 2 x 1.5 cm
Seed beads; peyote
PHOTO BY SARA TRO PHOTOGRAPHY

PATRICIA VENTURA PARRA
Cocoon Necklace ■ 2011

100 x 10 cm
Handmade Egyptian paste beads, handmade/thrown
Faenza clay elements, handmade wool beads, carded
wool, industrial felt string; fired, knotted, sewn
PHOTO BY ARTIST

LISA KLAKULAK
Incremental Metamorphosis ■ 2011

63.5 x 20.3 x 3.2 cm
Merino wool fleece, naturally dyed silk fabric, repurposed
brass wire, cotton sewing thread; needle felted, wet
felted, free-motion machine embroidered, hand stitched
PHOTO BY MARY VOGEL

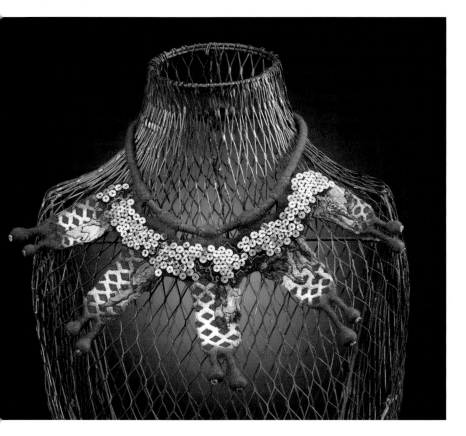

LISA KLAKULAK
Layers ■ 2010

21.6 x 27.9 x 3.8 cm
Merino wool fleece, Finn wool fleece, silk fabric, waxed
linen, cotton sewing thread, shell discs; needle felted, wet
felted, free-motion machine embroidered, hand stitched
PHOTOS BY STEVE MANN

LEY HOLLOWAY
Rock Pools Necklace ■ 2011

Dimensions unknown
Seed beads, sea glass, vintage
faceted beads; brick, beadweaving
PHOTO BY ARTIST

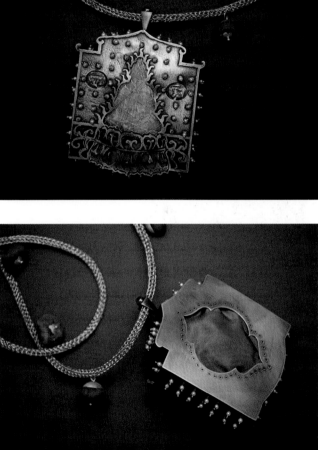

SUSAN YACOUB
Turquoise and Silver Leather Earrings ■ 2011
Each: 9 x 2.8 x 0.4 cm
Leather cabochons, crystals, metal, glass beads, seed beads,
suede-like backing; bead embroidery, peyote, edging, fringing
PHOTO BY OLLVIA YACOUB

LEAH MARIE HARDY
Flower: Fruit ■ 2011
46 x 10 x 1.5 cm
Silver, pearl beads, milkweed silk, cloth;
etched, soldered, wire-threaded, woven
PHOTOS BY ARTIST

PENNY ZOBEL
Where the Sea Meets the Shore ■ 2000
30 x 24.5 x 2.5 cm
Seed beads, found objects, seashells, bugle
beads; peyote, off-loom weaving, spiral
PHOTOS BY CHRIS AREND

JANET GRAFF
How Deep the Reef ■ 2011
39.4 x 39.4 x 1.3 cm
Lampworked beads, seed beads, charms,
commercial glass beads, shells, crystals; bead embroidery
PHOTO BY NATHANIEL GRAFF

361

KATHARINA EDER
Fadenspiel Magnetic Brooch ■ 2011

5 cm in diameter
Antique seed beads, polyamide
thread; bead crochet
PHOTO BY SIMONE ANDRESS

363

BRONWEN HEILMAN
Jazz Bracelet ■ 2010

3 x 18 cm
Glass beads, enamel, recycled bicycle inner
tube, rubber, sterling silver; flameworked
PHOTO BY DAVID ORR

STEPHANIE SERSICH
Juicy Colors Necklace ■ 2010

49 cm long
Handmade glass beads, handmade glass button,
Czech pressed-glass beads, Java glass beads,
wooden beads, resin beads, shells, floss, wax; knotted
PHOTO BY TOM EICHLER

MELISSA GRAKOWSKY
Sinusoidal Necklace ■ 2009
22.9 x 20.3 x 1.9 cm
Seed beads, crystal, glass
beads; herringbone, peyote
PHOTO BY ARTIST

GERLINDE LENZ
Herringbone with a Twist ■ 2010
54 x 4.5 cm
Cylinder beads, tiger's-eye doughnut, glass
pearl; tubular weave, flat Ndebele weave
PHOTO BY ARTIST

ADELE DENTON
Intertidal ■ 2011
30 x 30 x 2 cm
Seed beads, imperial jasper, freshwater
pearls; peyote, bead embroidery
PHOTO BY DANNY EVANS

367

TAMUNA LEZHAVA
Coral Reef ■ 2010

41 x 6 cm
Seed beads, Swarovski beads, artificial pearls, Murano
glass beads, chains, velvet ribbon; peyote variations

VANESSA WALILKO
Lilith the Snake ■ 2006

63.5 x 43 x 25 cm
Seed beads, brass wire, brass toggle
clasps; off-loom beadweaving, netting
PHOTO BY TREAVOR DOHERTY

MARY DIMATTEO
Golden Garden Necklace ■ 2010
47.5 cm long
Fire-polished beads, glass pearls, seed
beads, gold charlottes, snail beads,
gold-filled findings; spiral stitch variation
PHOTO BY ROBERT DIAMANTE

CARY FRANKLIN GASPAR
Moss Beaded Beads ■ 2009
68.6 x 6.4 x 1.3 cm
Seed beads, jade beads, Victorian
glass beads, sterling silver; freeform
right-angle weave, peyote
PHOTO BY TOM VAN EYNDE

SHERRY LEEDY
Necklace with Boingers ■ 1995

27.9 x 20.3 x 5.1 cm
Seed beads, glass beads; round peyote
PHOTO BY E.G. SCHEMPF

TOP
BARBARA FRY
Triangle Play: A Bracelet in Three Acts ■ 2010
25 x 3 x 1 cm
Bugle beads, cylinder beads, fire-polished crystals, clasp; peyote stitch
PHOTO BY SYNTHIA SIMON

BOTTOM
JEAN POWER
Geometric 2-8-1 (Collar for a Rangoli Girl) ■ 2008
47 x 18 x 4 cm
Seed beads, jump rings; peyote
PHOTO BY ARTIST

TERESA SULLIVAN
Gold Cone Earrings ■ 2010
Each: 5 x 2.5 x 1.5 cm
24-karat gold seed beads;
hollow-form sculptural peyote
PHOTO BY DAN KVITKA

CAROL WILCOX WELLS
Full Bloom ■ 2010
61 cm long
Seed beads, magatama beads, pearls, cubic
zirconia, gold-filled setting; right-angle weave
PHOTO BY STEVE MANN

AMY KATZ
The Wonder Wheel ▪ 2010

4 x 0.5 x 0.5 cm
Seed beads, crystals, glass
pearls, bugle beads; peyote
PHOTO BY CARRIE JOHNSON

MAUREEN CHIN
Crystal-Blue Medallion Ring ▪ 2011

30 x 30 x 30 cm
Japanese seed beads, Swarovski
crystals; off-loom beadweaving
PHOTO BY ARTIST

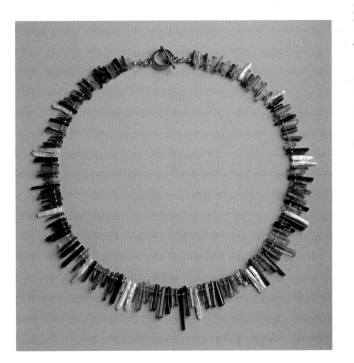

ETSUKO EDMONDS
Forest ■ 2011
19 x 16.5 cm
Tourmaline crystals, quartz, tourmaline
stems, pearl stems, sterling silver; strung

ETSUKO EDMONDS
Hanabana ■ 2011
20.5 x 16.5 cm
Tourmaline stems, pearl stems,
sterling silver; strung

SANDY LENT
Orange Anemone ■ 2009
5.1 x 40.7 x 0.6 cm
Acid-etched lampworked
beads, seed beads; strung
PHOTO BY RYDER GLEDHILL

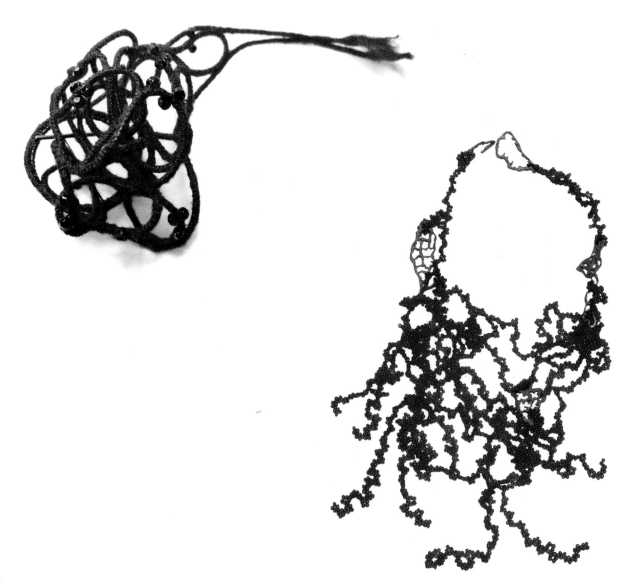

LUCIA NIEVES CORTÉS
Fire Brooch ■ 2009
15 x 6 x 5 cm
Czech glass beads, wool, thread,
silver; sewn, bead embroidery
PHOTO BY W. IMILAN

NORMA RINAUDO
Coral Reefs II ■ 2011
42 x 20 cm
Bronze, patina, glass beads; peyote, cast
PHOTO BY SOLEDAD TEJON

ANN TEVEPAUGH MITCHELL
Cloudy with Rain ■ 2007
26 x 18 x 1 cm
Seed beads, thread; peyote
PHOTO BY DEAN POWELL

SABINE LIPPERT
Renaissance Bracelet ■ 2011

1.9 x 19.1 cm
Seed beads, crystals, pearls
PHOTO BY ARTIST

VERONICA JONSSON
All-Pearl Necklace ■ 2010

45 cm long
Pearls; bead crochet
PHOTO BY MIKAEL HOLLSTEN

MELANIE POTTER

Honeycomb Lace ■ 2011

Various dimensions
Seed beads, pearls, French ear wire, rolo chain;
chevron chain, peyote, fringing, picots
PHOTO BY SCOTT POTTER

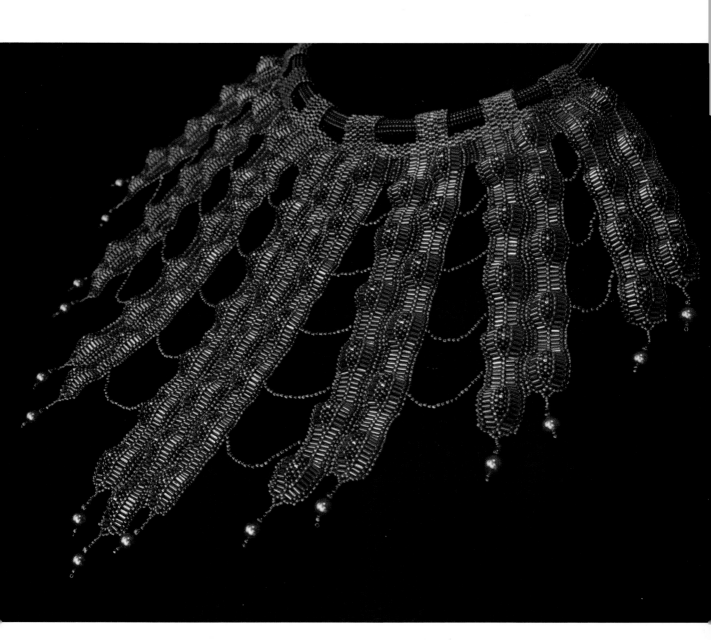

MET INNMON
Egyptian Waves Collar ■ 2008
29 x 31 x 0.8 cm
Bugle beads, seed beads, pearls;
peyote, herringbone, fringe
PHOTO BY LARRY HANSEN

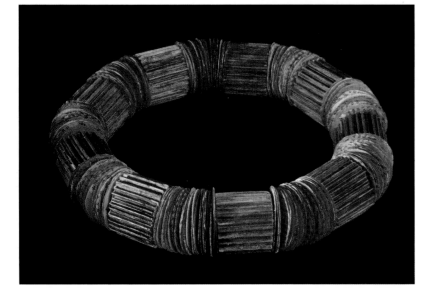

INGEBORG VANDAMME
Plant Necklace ■ 1996
20 x 20 x 4 cm
Plant, book pages, paraffin
PHOTO BY HENNI VAN BEEK

LYNNE SAUSELE
Michelle Beaded-Bead Necklace ■ 2010
50 x 2.5 x 2.5 cm
Seed beads, Swarovski crystals; peyote
PHOTO BY ROBERT DIAMANTE

HUIB PETERSEN
Celtic Basket-Weave Necklace ■ 2007

50 cm long
Seed beads; tubular right-angle weave
PHOTO BY ARTIST

PATRICIA ZABRESKI
Ancient Urn ■ 2009

55.9 x 2.5 x 1.3 cm
Handmade etched lampworked glass
beads, lampworked urn, Swarovski crystals
PHOTO BY JERRY ANTHONY

FACING PAGE LEFT
ANITA SPENCER
Study in Brown, Black, and Ivory ■ 2010

45 x 2 x 1.3 cm
Soda-lime glass, silver toggle clasp,
sterling-silver saucer beads
PHOTO BY JERRY ANTHONY

TOP RIGHT
MELANIE MOERTEL
White Islands Bracelet ■ 2011

21.5 cm long
Lampworked beads, silk ribbon, sterling silver
PHOTO BY ARTIST

BOTTOM RIGHT
LESLEE FRUMIN
Calypso Cuff ■ 2008

4.1 x 19.1 cm
Japanese seed beads, semiprecious
beads, pearls, sterling-silver clasp,
sterling-silver wire; ladder, brick, peyote
PHOTO BY HAP SAKWA

ADELE DENTON
Queen Lydia ■ 2011

60 x 30 x 2 cm
Kingman turquoise, carnelian, seed beads, pearls, Swarovski
crystal, leather; peyote stitch, brick stitch, embroidery
PHOTO BY DANNY EVANS

NANCY CAIN
Cain's Chain ■ 2007
50 x 1.5 cm
Seed beads, crystals, crystal pearls; hollow
beaded beads, tubular peyote rope
PHOTO BY DAVE WOLVERTON

CAROL WILCOX WELLS
Cone Flower and Pearls ■ 2010
96.5 cm long
Seed beads, magatama beads, crystal rice pearls,
stick pearls; right-angle weave, loop bezel
PHOTOS BY STEVE MANN

387

JOANN BAUMANN
Fluffy Fiesta ■ 2011
22 x 16 x 5 cm
Seed beads, triangle beads; peyote
PHOTO BY LARRY SANDERS

KYUNGHEE KIM
Dancing Tree Neckpiece ■ 2010
75 x 6 x 0.7 cm
Wooden beads
PHOTO BY KWANGCHUN PARK

SHERRY SERAFINI
Carnival ■ 2010
19.1 x 7.6 x 1.3 cm
Raku, glass, cabochons,
seed beads; bead embroidery
PHOTOS BY ARTIST

FACING PAGE
TATYANA FEDORIKHINA
Venice Beach ■ 2010
10 x 21 x 23 cm
Coral beads, seed beads, glass beads, silk,
nylon, leather cord; micro macramé, peyote
PHOTO BY JENNIFER PARKER

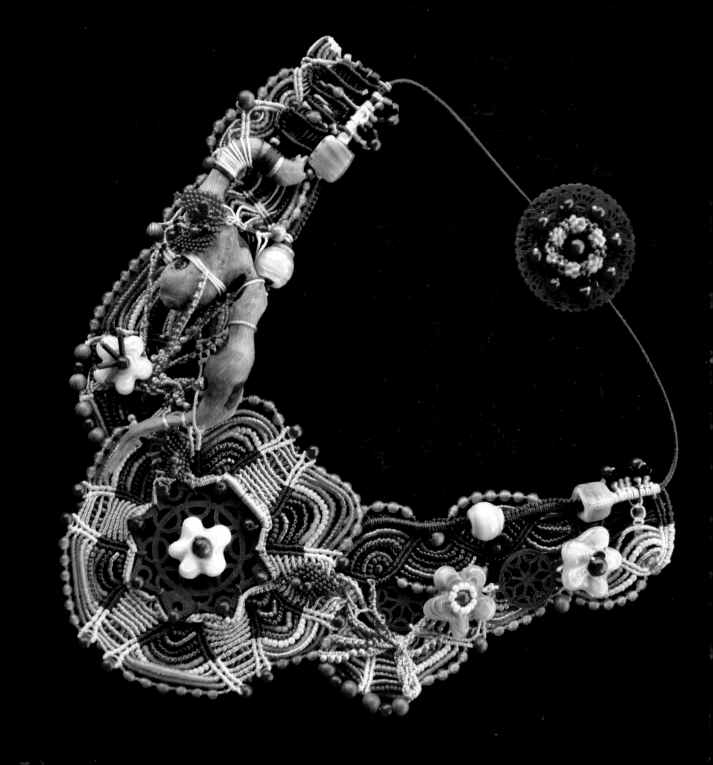

NOMFUNDO CEBEKHULU
Mafu Necklace ■ 2010

30 x 43.5 x 0.3 cm
Sterling silver, opaque glass beads, nylon thread; brick
PHOTO BY ANDREW GRIFFIN

AVA EDMONDS
Maru ■ 2011
18.5 cm
Turquoise shell, Roman glass, antique seed
glass, sterling silver; strung, wire wrapped
PHOTO BY MARTIN BARKER

MEGAN ISAACS
Penny Necktie ■ 2011
36 x 12 x 2 cm
Oxidized pennies, oxidized
brass, chainmail; fabricated
PHOTO BY ARTIST

ADI CLOETE
Royal Red Necklace ■ 2009
Pendant: 9.8 x 4.6 cm
Silver, garnets, seed beads, glass beads;
hand fabricated, engraved, peyote

ELHADJI KOUMAMA
Tuareg Fancy Silver Chatchat Necklace ■ 2010
40 x 5 x 0.2 cm
Fine silver, black onyx; hand engraved

TOP
SHERRY LEEDY
Red Coral and Pearl Bracelet ■ 2010

12.1 x 12.1 x 3.8 cm
Seed beads, red coral, pearls,
glass beads; round peyote
PHOTOS BY E.G. SCHEMPF

KATHRYN BOWMAN
Scarlet Crescent ■ 2009

19.1 x 1.6 cm
Czech fire-polished glass beads, Bali silver beads, sterling-silver
box clasp, sterling-silver wire, beaded beads; bead crochet
PHOTO BY ANNIE PENNINGTON

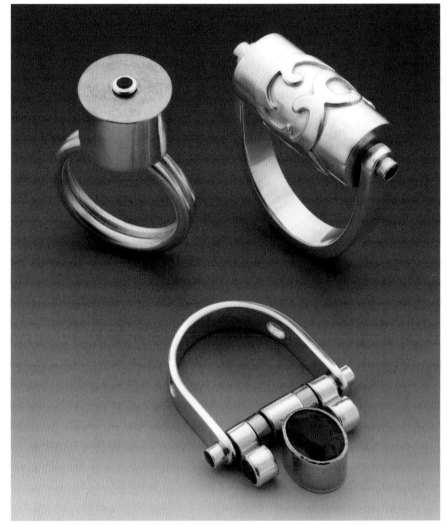

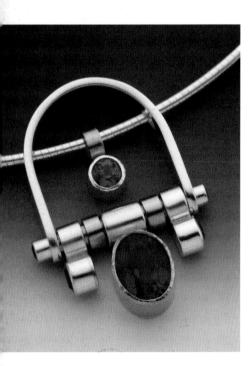

KATHLEEN E. WADE
Revolutionaries: Spinning Bead Rings ■ 2011

Left: 3 x 3 x 1.3 cm; right: 3 x 3 x 1.2 cm; bottom: 3.2 x 2.4 x 0.7 cm
22-karat gold, 18-karat gold, Argentium sterling silver, sterling silver, sapphire, garnet, citrine; fabricated, pierced, fused, riveted, textured, bezel set
PHOTOS BY GEORGE POST

BETSY YOUNGQUIST
Eye Flower Pins ■ 2009
Each: 3.9 x 3.9 x 1.3 cm
Seed beads, bugle beads, vintage glass
stones, antique glass doll eyes; mosaic
PHOTO BY LARRY SANDERS

397

GALATEA KONTOS
Impression: Black ■ 2011
Each: 11.5 x 4 x 0.5 cm
Paper, copper, seed beads, embroidery floss,
sterling silver; fabricated, oxidized, strung
PHOTO BY SARA BROWN

CAROLINE GORE
...after... ■ 2011
30 x 19.5 x 2 cm
18-karat gold, sterling silver, jet, reclaimed leather,
borosilicate glass, hematite, silk; oxidized
PHOTO BY ARTIST

BIANCA EDMONDS
Face of the Moon Necklace ■ 2011

25 x 14 cm
Porcelain, sterling silver, labradorite, rainbow moonstone,
seed beads; hand sculpted, etched, constructed, crimp and wire
PHOTOS BY MARTIN BARKER

NANCY MELI WALKER
Beads of Silicone ■ 2011
24 x 18 cm
Sterling silver, silicone, silk;
fabricated, kumihimo braiding

ANDREW COSTEN
Lunar Orbit ■ 2011

26 cm long
Lava beads, sterling-silver rondelles; cylinder bur texture
PHOTO BY SARAH-HANNAH BEDARD

ALIKI STROUMPOULI
Ping Pong ■ 2011

43 x 10 x 3.5 cm
Ping-pong balls; embroidery
PHOTO BY ARTIST

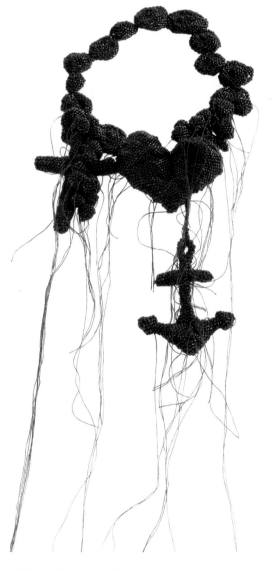

KATHARINA EDER
Fadenspiel ■ 2011

25 cm in diameter
Seed beads, polyamide
thread; bead crochet
PHOTO BY SIMONE ANDRESS

ARIANNE VAN DER GAAG
Untitled ■ 2010

32 cm long
Glass beads; strung
PHOTO BY RENS HORN

Showcase 500
beaded jewelry

ANNETA VALIOUS
Eos ■ 2011
26 x 15 x 2 cm
Quartz rose, pearls, crystals, seed beads,
soutache braid; soutache embroidery
PHOTOS BY ARTIST

CARMEN ANDERSON
Beetle Love ■ 2008
54.6 cm long
Polymer clay, rubber, metallic powder

CARLA BRONZINI
Collana Ricamo Nero ■ 2010
21 x 17 x 1 cm
Seed beads, crystals, stone,
onyx, fabric; bead embroidery

INGER MARIE BERG
Darkness Necklace ■ 2010

45 cm long
Sterling silver, plastic, hematite,
glass beads; hand fabricated
PHOTO BY ARTIST

405

KATHY KING
Forest Embroidered Necklace ■ 2010

48.3 x 6.4 x 0.6 cm
Seed beads, Czech glass, crystals,
glass pearls; bead embroidery, quilling
PHOTO BY JASON DOWDLE

NOME MAY
White Rose Necklace ■ 2007
Rose centerpiece: 5 x 6 x 0.5 cm
Antique seed beads, pearls,
tourmaline, silver; bead embroidery
PHOTO BY MARTIN KILMER

407

D. JEKA LAMBERT
Convertible Necklace Silver and Gold ■ 2011
65 x 4 cm
Seed beads, 24-karat gold-plated beads, glass
beads, nylon thread; peyote, ladder, brick, fringe
PHOTO BY YVETTE TAYLOR

MAYRA NIEVES-BEKELE
Bronze Dragon ■ 2010
31 x 16 x 1.5 cm
Seed beads, Swarovski pearls, glass beads;
right-angle weave, freeform peyote
PHOTO BY GEORGE POST

MAGGIE MEISTER
Castellani Necklace ■ 2009

25.4 x 26.7 x 1.3 cm
Carved scarabs, seed beads;
square, brick, peyote
PHOTO BY GEORGE POST

409

MARGIE DEEB
Troy Collar ■ 2008
22 x 12 cm
Pressed glass, 24-karat gold-plated
seed beads, glass seed beads; stringing
PHOTO BY ARTIST

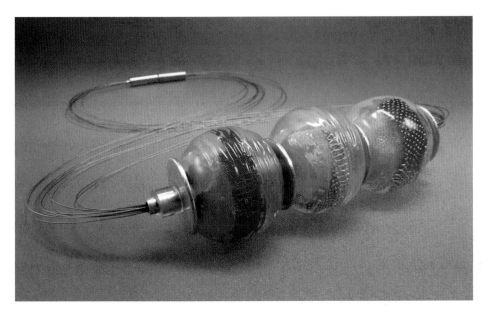

MANUELA WUTSCHKE
Triptychon ■ 2011

50 cm long
Soft glass beads, sterling
silver, stainless steel
PHOTO BY ARTIST

VERONICA JONSSON
Colorful Intentions ■ 2011

2 x 16 cm
Glass pearls, crystal, seed beads,
fringe drop beads; brick
PHOTO BY MIKAEL HOLLSTEN

TAMUNA LEZHAVA
Yellow-Green Passion ■ 2011

80 x 4 cm
Seed beads, Swarovski beads and crystals, chains, metal-covered beads, silk ribbons, organza ribbons; right-angle weave, tubular Ndebele, square, square Ndebele
PHOTO BY VAKHTANG ALANIA

KIRA SEIDEN
Cube Necklace ■ 2010
83.5 cm long
Glass, wax; fused, ground
PHOTO BY ARTIST

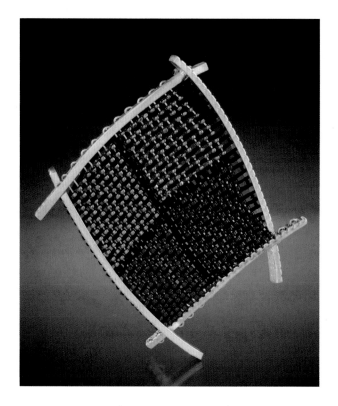

SHARON M. DONOVAN
Four-Square Brooch ■ 2011
7.6 x 6.3 cm
Sterling silver, glass beads,
silk thread; fabricated, woven
PHOTO BY LARRY SANDERS

LAURA MCCABE
Rainbow Calsilica Eiffel Tower Bracelet ■ 2010
17 x 2.5 x 2.5 cm
Custom-cut rainbow calsilica points, seed beads, freshwater
pearls, sterling-silver clasp; herringbone, peyote, embellishment
PHOTO BY MELINDA HOLDEN

RACHEL NELSON-SMITH
O. Bersten Specimen ■ 2008

51 x 38 x 1.5 cm
Glass, crystal, nylon, gold;
right-angle weave, peyote
MADE WITH THE ASSISTANCE OF LIZ PENN
PHOTO BY ARTIST

JAN HULING
Butterflies ■ 2011
48.3 x 2.5 cm
Seed beads, metal, grout; glued
PHOTO BY PHIL HULING

Showcase 500
beaded jewelry

RACHEL NELSON-SMITH
Vigo Cuff ■ 2009
9 x 18 x 0.5 cm
Glass, crystal, nylon, leather; bead embroidery
PHOTO BY ARTIST

417

AURELIO CASTAÑO
Winter Pond Ring ■ 2011

3.8 cm in diameter
Rivoli beads, Japanese seed beads, Swarovski pearls
and crystals, Delica beads; round peyote, netting

PHOTOS BY JAMES KATT

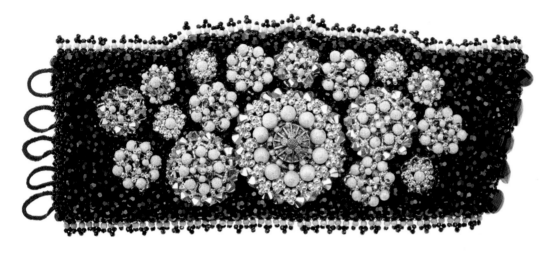

YVONNE BAUGHMAN
Jenna's Bridal Cuff ■ 2011

7.5 x 18 x 2.5 cm
Crystals, silver beads, seed beads, new and vintage
buttons; bead embroidery, right-angle weave
PHOTO BY SCOTT VAN OSDOL

YVONNE BAUGHMAN
Garden of Pearls ■ 2011

8.5 x 20 x 2 cm
Crystal beads, pearls, vintage button,
seed beads; bead embroidery
PHOTO BY SCOTT VAN OSDOL

419

MARGO C. FIELD
Ornamental Rivoli Necklace ■ 2011
17 x 13 x 1.3 cm
Seed beads, rivoli bead, crystals, glass pearls,
mother-of-pearl beads; peyote, herringbone, netting
PHOTOS BY PAT BERRETT

Showcase 500
beaded jewelry

CAROL WILCOX WELLS
Season's End ■ 2010

50.8 cm long
Seed beads, magatama beads,
pearls; right-angle weave
PHOTO BY STEVE MANN

BETTY STEPHAN
Twilight ■ 2011

28 x 18 cm
Stone cabochons, vintage earrings, glass
beads, seed beads; bead embroidery
PHOTO BY TIM FUSS

HEIDI KUMMLI
Shapeshifter ■ 2010

45.7 x 8.9 x 5.1 cm
Seed beads, dagger beads, cabochons,
bronze feather, fur; bead embroidery
PHOTOS BY ARTIST

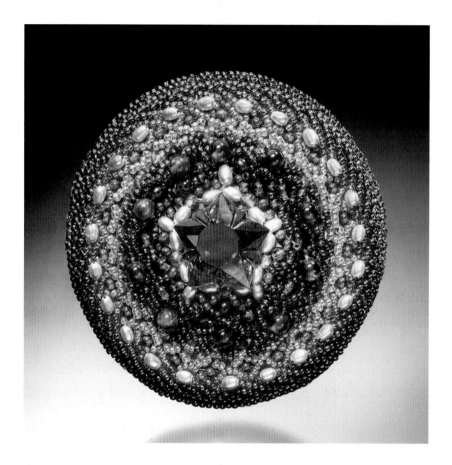

DIXIE GABRIC
Colors of My Ever After ■ 2010

21 x 15 cm
Bronze turquoise, amethyst cabochons, seed
beads; peyote, backstitch, bead embroidery
PHOTO BY JEFF GABRIC

ANDREA L. STERN
A Trip to the Moon ■ 2008

30 x 12 x 1 cm
Seed beads, ceramic element, pressed
glass; right-angle weave, peyote
PHOTO BY MARTIN STERN

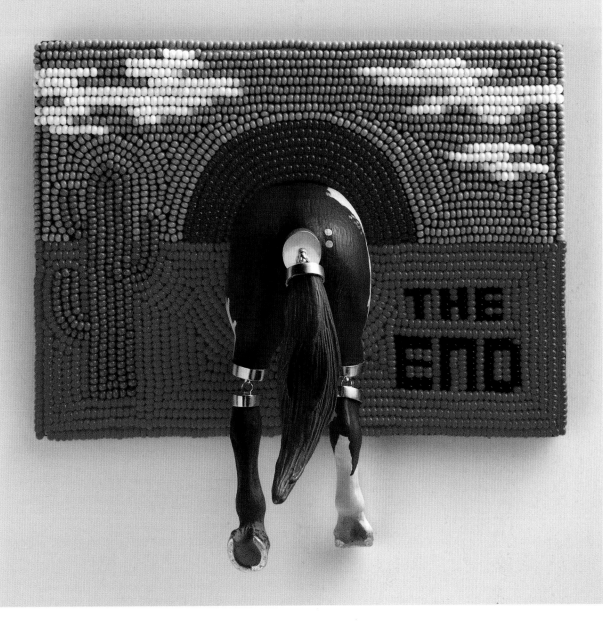

FELIEKE VAN DER LEEST
The End 1 ■ 2011
4 x 12 cm
Seed beads, plastic animal, silver;
bead embroidery, metalsmithing
PHOTO BY EDDO HARTMANN

contributing artists

Showcase 500
beaded jewelry

acknowledgments

My deepest thanks go to the beadwork artists who submitted images of their best pieces for this beautiful volume. This community of artists is exceptionally generous with themselves and their talents, and it is always both a joy and a privilege to be part of this vibrant community and to be working in support of it.

At Lark Books and Lark Jewelry & Beading, I want to give an extra loud shout out to Dawn Dillingham. I've worked as senior editor on more than 18 gallery books, and Dawn's contributions in editorial have been an integral part of each and every one of them. Some books reach a moment where, for a multiplicity of reasons, they either are or aren't going to happen. Dawn made this book happen.

In much the same way, editor Julie Hale's contributions to virtually all of Lark's gallery books since the beginning of 2007, when I first started working here, can't be overstated. Julie brings her editorial excellence, graceful turn of phrase, and true diligence to all these books, and in so doing she makes all the difference in their quality.

Also contributing to this project in varied and important ways were Matt Shay, Kathy Holmes, Carol Morse Barnao, Kay Holmes Stafford, Hannah Doyle, Abby Haffelt, Nathalie Mornu, Todd Kaderabek, Lance Wille, Kathy Sheldon, Shannon Yokeley, Gavin Young, Wolf Hoelscher, Simone Gibbs, and Jeff Batzli. My sincere gratitude to everyone: You do outstanding work, and you make my job lots of fun.

Finally, thank you to my children: to my daughters, Danaelle and Layla, and to my son, Nicholas. I love you.

— **Ray Hemachandra**

about the author

Author and juror Ray Hemachandra is the team lead and business manager for Lark Jewelry & Beading. His books as author or senior editor include *The Penland Book of Glass; Beading with World Beads; Masters: Beadweaving* and other Masters Series books, including *Masters: Gold, Masters: Blown Glass, Masters: Polymer Clay, Masters: Earthenware*, and the first and second volumes of *Masters: Art Quilts*; and numerous books in the 500 Series, including *500 Judaica, 500 Art Quilts, 500 Vases, 500 Raku*, and three furniture books in the series devoted to chairs, tables, and cabinets. As a senior editor working with leading beading teachers and authors, he launched Lark's best-selling Beadweaving Master Class series. He lives in Asheville, North Carolina.

31901051532358

ÉVA DOBOS
Rinde Bracelet ■ 2011
1.5 cm, 9 cm in diameter
Imitation pearls, seed beads, fire-polished
beads, pressed glass beads, Delica beads,
fire-polished donuts; embellishment
PHOTO BY SANDON BODOGAN